RumRill Pottery

the Ohio Years

1938–1942
identification and value guide

Francesca Fisher

PHOTOGRAPHY BY
Carl Fisher

COLLECTOR BOOKS
A Division of Schroeder Publishing Co., Inc.

Front cover, upper row, left to right:
H-10 vase, Forest Green, 9½", $30.00 – 65.00, depending on glaze.
RumRill Dealer sign (unmarked), Sea Spray Green, 8", $150.00 – 300.00, depending on glaze.
RumRill nude (unmarked), Deep Matte Blue, 7½", $75.00 – 200.00, depending on glaze.

Lower row, left to right:
I-3 vase, Forest Fire, 10", $40.00 – 75.00, depending on glaze.
Salt and pepper shaker set with original gold and black RumRill labels, Gentian Blue and Tangerine, 2½", $50.00.
C-2 vase, Dubonnet, 4", $15.00 – 30.00.
E-12 low bulb bowl, Cadet Blue, 7" diameter, $10.00 – 15.00, depending on glaze.
E-5 vase, Daffodil, 6", $10.00 – 15.00.
L-7 Modern Head vase, Parisian White, 11", $300.00 – 500.00, depending on glaze.

Back cover, upper row, left to right:
J-35 vase, Sea Spray Green, $20.00 – 75.00.
505 vase, Neptune Green, 16", $250.00– 300.00.

Lower row, left to right:
F-20 flowerpot, Daffodil Yellow, 5½", $25.00 – 30.00.
R-101 pig planter, Parisian White, 2½", $35.00 – 50.00.
B-10 bird, Cadet Blue, 3¼", $15.00 – 20.00.
Butterfly planter, Parisian White, 9", $500.00.
P-3 creamer, Forest Fire, 4", $35.00 – 50.00.
J-34 vase, Cameo, 10", $75.00 – 80.00.

Cover design by Beth Summers
Book design by Terri Hunter
Photography by Carl Fisher

COLLECTOR BOOKS
P.O. Box 3009
Paducah, Kentucky 42002-3009

www.collectorbooks.com

The current values in this book should be used only as a guide. They are not intended to set prices, which vary from one section of the country to another. Auction prices as well as dealer prices vary greatly and are affected by condition as well as demand. Neither the author nor the publisher assume responsibility for any losses that might be incurred as a result of consulting this guide.

Searching for a Publisher?

We are always looking for people knowledgeable within their fields. If you feel that there is a real need for a book on your collectible subject and have a large comprehensive collection, contact Collector Books.

Contents

RUMRILL
Pottery Company
"Every Piece Built For A Purpose"
LITTLE ROCK
ARKANSAS

Acknowledgments

We wish to thank the many, many people that provided information for this book, especially the Ohio Historical Society and the Morrow County Historical Society, who preserved the original letters, catalogs, and documents that were necessary in order to complete this book.

In addition, my fellow colleague and longtime collector friend, Joseph Brawley of Ravenna, Ohio, collaborated with me and provided insightful knowledge and timelines. Without his help, this book would not have been possible. Pieces from his 500+ collection are featured throughout this book, and, as you will see, some of these pieces are experimental and/or were never featured in any catalog.

Personal interviews were granted by Katherine Kline, Claudia McLain, Harold "Dutch" West, Louise Bauer, Ray Reiss, Harvey Duke, Ron Hoopes, David Edwin Gifford, Myrna Wall, Joseph Brawley, Harry O. Rumrill, and Evelyn Taylor.

Correspondence with Jim Pfeifer, Robert Zaeske, Louise T. Jones, Georgine J. Mickler, Gertrude Sellers Rumrill, Barbara Borck, Roger Sexter, Byron Bush, Mark Ebertowski, George Irving, the Ohio Historical Society, and others also provided valuable information. My personal collection of RumRill pottery would not have been possible without the help of antique dealers who were always scouting for me, including Phil Shimola, Steve Aldred, Walter Hogan, and others.

A special thanks goes to John Stadnicki for his role in securing some important documents that were needed for this book, and to Stark Beard who kept in touch and interviewed several factory workers from the Florence Pottery Company.

My indispensable assistant, Mandy Hogan, played a key part in retyping the notes that were taken 30 years ago when I first started documenting the history of RumRill pottery.

Lastly, I wish to thank my husband Carl for making my life's dream possible. Without his patience, understanding, and encouragement, this book would have never been possible. Carl photographed the amazing pieces that you will see throughout this book.

I'm a great believer that, in business, you have to give back to the community. For me, this is the opportunity to share my knowledge of the past 30 years with you, my fellow collector. Once you hold a piece of RumRill pottery in your hands, you will realize that you are holding something very rare — something that was made for only four years, from 1938 to 1942.

I hope you will enjoy reading this book and learning about RumRill pottery. If you have a particular piece from your collection that you would like identified, or possibly included in my next book, please write to me at the RumRill Society, Box 2161, Hudson, OH 44236. Or, you are welcome to call me on my toll-free number, 1-888-RUMRILL.

Good luck and good finds!

Francesca Fisher

About the Author

Francesca Fisher has been a collector of RumRill pottery for over 30 years. She has devoted most of her life to finding out as much as she could about RumRill pottery.

Before eBay, Fisher would travel all over the country looking for pieces to add to her 800+ piece collection. Even after the internet came about, she still could not find any information about RumRill pottery that was made after 1938.

In 1996, she formed the *RumRill Society,* which was a short-lived newsletter that was devoted to sharing information to other collectors about the little-known time period of RumRill. In search of more information, and to get answers to questions that were asked of her, she took out countless classified ads in local newspapers throughout mid-Ohio in hopes that people associated with the Florence Pottery Company or RumRill Pottery could provide answers. Many people came forward, and because of their help, this book was possible.

Fisher worked in collaboration with poetry author and major RumRill collector Joseph Brawley, and the two shared their information and printed literature about RumRill's four-year production period. Brawley is considered one of the top five collectors in the United States, and his collection exceeds 1,000 pieces. He is also considered an authority on RumRill pottery.

Fisher owns and operates three businesses in Ohio: Body Sculpting by Exterior Designs, Inc., Geri-Fit Co. Ltd., and Professional Auction Listing Service. She is a monthly fitness columnist and writes for several Ohio newspapers. She is also a freelance writer for national health and fitness magazines, and antique newspapers, and she is a frequent presenter at trade shows and conventions.

In addition to running these companies, Fisher has starred in and produced a line of body sculpting fitness videos and DVDs, including the "Geri-Fit" fitness program for older adults; "Weights I, II, and III"; "Phenomenal Abdominals"; "Teen-Fit"; "Back-Fit with Pilates"; "Just Legs"; "Stretch This"; and "Golf-Fit", all of which she sells on her website, www.flexcity.com.

Fisher's background includes 40 years of writing and 25 years experience in strength training. She is a former international competitive bodybuilder and title holder, and has served as a member of the National Strength and Conditioning Association Advisory Committee. She has also authored three books on the subject of strength training. In 1998, she was chosen as one of Cleveland's Top 10 Women Business Owners by the local chapter of the National Association of Women Business Owners.

She lives in Aurora, Ohio, with her husband, Carl, an engineer and contemporary marble artist.

Introduction

Who is George Rumrill and why has he become a legend in the modern day world of art pottery? George Rumrill was a visionary and his work stands today as a testimony to his remarkable abilities. With his early appearance at Red Wing Potteries in 1932 through 1938, and the four years to follow through 1942, one can only assume that a pottery made for this short period of time could easily be construed as "collectible."

No one really knows how many pieces of RumRill were ever produced. The supply, having only been manufactured for 12 years (mostly at Red Wing from 1932 to 1938), is very limited. But, even more limited was the time that RumRill was made in Ohio, from 1938 to 1942. This book represents this period in history.

The value of RumRill pottery should not be mistaken for ordinary, everyday pottery, especially since production was very limited due to George Rumrill's early death in 1943. RumRill pottery represents a turning point in history which can never be replaced.

As you read about the history and the making of RumRill pottery, remember that you have found something special in RumRill. This pottery from the past, left to us by George Rumrill, is an inspirational experience that words cannot describe. I hope that you will have the opportunity to own RumRill pottery and that you will begin to enjoy the grace and energy it can bring to your life.

This RumRill vase appeared on the cover of the July/August 1993 issue of the *Journal of the American Art Pottery Association*. The article, written by Michael R. Zaeske, discusses the history of RumRill pottery.

The Collection

When I moved in 2000, I had to pack up my entire collection. What a pain that was. Needless to say, I kept most of it boxed since that move. I hadn't realized how many more pieces I had accumulated all these years until I began to unpack them for this shoot. My basement quickly turned into a "vasement!"

On the pages to follow are pieces from my collection, which were photographed based on their finishes. The collection starts with Cadet Blue, followed by Stipple Blue, Gentian Blue, Mandarin Blue, Forest Fire, Cameo (peach), Daffodil Yellow, Forest Green, the Ohio RumRill nudes, Dubonnet and Burgundy Red, Sea Spray Green, Parisian White, Ashes of Roses, Shawnee-made Sea Spray Green, and Neptune Green.

Enjoy!

Cadet Blue.

Cadet Blue.

Stipple Blue, Gentian Blue, and Mandarin Blue.

Forest Fire.

Cameo (peach).

Daffodil Yellow.

Forest Green.

Ohio RumRill nudes.

Dubonnet and Burgundy Red.

Sea Spray Green.

Sea Spray Green.

Parisian White.

Parisian White.

Ashes of Roses.

Shawnee-made Sea Spray Green.

Neptune Green.

VOLUME 30, NO. 5 MAY, 1938

GLASS · · · · ENAMEL · · · · POTTERY

CERAMIC INDUSTRY

WORLD'S LEADING CERAMIC JOURNAL

The History of RumRill Pottery

George Djalma Rumrill was born in Gainesville, Texas, on January 29, 1881. Not much is known as to how or why he started in the pottery business. At the time he was 32 years old, he was working as a manager at the Pulaski Ice Company in Little Rock, Arkansas. His sister, Edith Frances Rumrill, also worked there.

In 1926, George Rumrill worked as a sales manager at the Louis Schneider Candy Company, also of Little Rock, Arkansas. His sister also followed him there and worked as the company's secretary.

Sometime in early 1930, George Rumrill founded the Arkansas Products Company. The company supposedly distributed pottery for Camark and Niloak. George Rumrill's position was a salesman and sales manager. His sister was also working at the company as its secretary. It is believed that Rumrill's wife was also involved with the business.

RumRill had its own line of pottery which was very short-lived. It was only made for about ten years, from 1932 – 1942. It was never manufactured in Arkansas, but several pottery companies made RumRill for George, including Red Wing Potteries, Shawnee, Florence, and Gonder.

In 1931, Red Wing was trying to get away from the utilitarian line of crockware it was manufacturing and wanted to get into a more decorative line of vases.

George Rumrill had made an agreement with the Red Wing Pottery Company to produce a line of art pottery vases and other items under the tradename "RUMRILL" for probably an initial five-year period. During the time at Red Wing, vases and other items were incised with the "RUMRILL" mark and a three-digit shape number, except for some pitchers and cups, which were marked with a two-digit shape number.

In trademark records, we found that Red Wing Union Stoneware Company filed for trademark protection for the trademark "Rum Rill." The mark was published for opposition in the *Trademark Gazette* on November 26, 1935.

In researching further, we found that George Rumrill assigned his "RUMRILL" trademark to Red Wing Potteries later in 1936. The "RUMRILL" trademark was already registered under trademark record #330010, and the mark was owned by George Rumrill and then partner Alfred Leymer of the RumRill Pottery Company, which was on record at being located at 1213 Broadway, Little Rock, Arkansas. Both George Rumrill and his sister, Edith Frances Rumrill, signed the assignment papers giving full title and rights to the "RUMRILL" mark to Red Wing Potteries on May 27, 1936.

Perhaps Rumrill tried to "save face" and instituted an alternate plan, sensing the end of the Red Wing era was near. This forced Rumrill to find another manufacturer to produce his pottery line. He started sending out letters in order to recruit a team of designers, and these letters were sent as early as October of 1937. Sure enough, in 1938, Red Wing announced that it was planning to discontinue the RumRill line but would continue producing the line without Rumrill or his trade name on the pieces.

A press release appearing in the May 1938 issue of *Ceramic Industry* states that "the trademarks have been assigned to the RumRill Pottery Company."

It is the belief of this author that Red Wing Potteries and George Rumrill settled a pending trademark dispute in an out-of-court settlement. Red Wing continued to produce the same vases for a short time thereafter, but without the RumRill mark. It was Red Wing's intention to phase out the art pottery line altogether and develop its own line of practical vases with an entirely new modern look. Soon thereafter, Charles Murphy and Belle Kogan went on to become two of the top designers in Red Wing Pottery's history.

Some of the people that I interviewed said that George Rumrill was planning to leave Red Wing anyway because it was time for him to start producing his own line of pottery. It was said that the Shawnee Pottery Company came in at a lower bid and Rumrill left Red Wing in order to go over to Shawnee.

Rumrill Pottery To Make Own Ware

According to a recent announcement by George D. Rumrill, sales manager of the Rumrill Pottery Co., Little Rock, Ark., that company is now making ware at Zanesville, Ohio. This organization was formerly a part of the Red Wing (Minn.) Potteries, Inc., which, at that time, owned the name RumRill. Now, however, all rights, titles, interests, claims and trade-marks of the Rumrill name have been assigned to the Rumrill Pottery Co. Red Wing Potteries has the right to dispose of all pottery in either bisque or finished state with that name on it, but they cannot manufacture any more under that trade-mark.

Press release appearing in the May 1938 issue of *Ceramic Industry.*

The History of RumRill Pottery

It is believed that Shawnee manufactured RumRill pottery as early as April 2, 1938, until the end of that year.

It is a general consensus and belief amongst collectors and art pottery historians that Rumrill broke off his association with Shawnee because of an ongoing problem with vases leaking water. This presented a great problem because most of RumRill's customers at that time were floral shops.

If you compare the RumRill pottery made by Red Wing to the RumRill pottery made at Shawnee, you will notice a big difference in the quality. Not only are the finishes distinctly different, but the look, feel, and durability are, too. And when you compare the Shawnee-made RumRill to that of the Florence-made RumRill, the decrease in quality is even more apparent. This is not to say that post-Red Wing RumRills are a poor investment; it simply means certain pieces made at certain times are more likely to appreciate in value than others.

However, it is this author's opinion that, after researching and comparing price catalogs from this era, it was evident that the Shawnee-made RumRill pottery wares were very expensive for their time. This probably meant that there was a very small profit margin for George Rumrill if he continued to stay at Shawnee.

For example, the "F" series of the vases are listed at $9.60 per dozen in the Shawnee RumRill catalog, whereas the same "F" series is priced at $4.80 per dozen in the Florence RumRill catalog. Perhaps the lack of waterproofing was just an excuse to break the contract with Shawnee Pottery, but Rumrill left nonetheless.

Not too far away was Mt. Gilead, Ohio — home of the Florence Pottery Company. Named after Florence Haserodt Gray, the Florence Pottery Company manufactured clay pottery, flowerpots, and clay tiles. Prior to it being named the Florence Pottery Company, it was called the McGowan and Company Pottery, then the Mt. Gilead Tile and Clay Works. Business and historical records date the start of the McGowan Pottery Company at around 1888. At that time, McGowan manufactured drain tiles, jugs, crocks, and canning jars.

Florence was a smaller, more personalized pottery company whose new board of directors became quickly entranced by RumRill and his business plan to take his pottery line national and international. William F. Bruce, president of Florence Pottery Company, died on November 15, 1938, and his son, J. Ewart Bruce, soon thereafter became president.

In an article dated December 1, 1938, that appeared in the *Morrow County Sentinental*, the headlines read, "POTTERY TO MAKE NEW LINE HERE," "New Equipment And Added Force to Begin Next Month," "Discontinue Pots," "RUMRILL Art Ware To Be Only Product of Remodeled Plant." The article mentioned that the Florence Pottery Company would "discontinue the manufacture of the red flowerpots which have been the principal product of the company for several years and will engage in a new manufacturing line."

Florence upgraded its kiln, and employed creative glazers and finishers. They began hiring 50 to 60 more people to work at the plant in anticipation of securing the contract with the RumRill Pottery Company. They also hired general manager Lawton Gonder. Gonder was in charge of the reconstruction of the plant so that the new equipment could be immediately installed, in addition to improving the equipment that was presently used to make pottery. He was also to serve as the person in charge of production. According to the newspaper article, prior to working at the Florence Pottery Company, Gonder worked at the American Encaustic Tile Company in Zanesville, Ohio, for about 20 years, and later with the Fraunfelter China Company.

The first order on record with the Florence Pottery Company producing items for the RumRill Pottery Company is dated January 15, 1939. From that point forward, Lawton Gonder and George Rumrill formed a relationship that would carry the RumRill name for another three years. The RumRill Pottery Company continued to be based out of Little Rock,

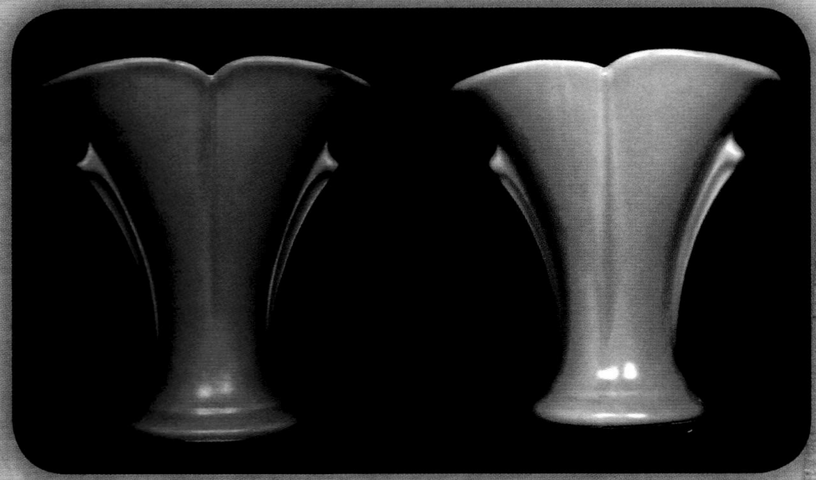

When Rumrill broke off his association with Shawnee, this was one of the few molds he took over to the Florence Pottery Company. The Shawnee-made RumRill is on the left. Shawnee-made RumRill vases are often signed with the double-r mark. The Florence-made RumRill is on the right. Notice the differences in the finish colors and glazes. The Shawnee-made RumRill is more defined and the finish is very distinct. Florence-made RumRills have a thicker glaze and the mold lines were not very crisp. Both makers are very easy to distinguish once you familiarize yourself with the finishes and feel of the pottery.

Florence Pottery, ca. 1930.

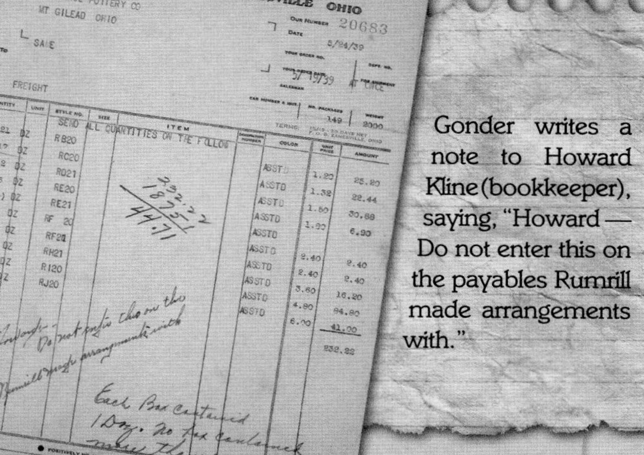
ORIGINAL INVOICE

SHAWNEE POTTERY COMPANY

OFFICE AND WORKS — ZANESVILLE OHIO

Sold To: FLORENCE POTTERY CO, MT GILEAD OHIO

SALE

Our Number 20683

Date 5/24/39

Via FREIGHT

No. Packages 149 — Weight 2000

Quantity	Unit	Style No.	Item	Color	Unit Price	Amount
		SEND	ALL QUANTITIES ON THE FOLLOW			
21	DZ	RB20		ASSTD	1.20	25.20
17	DZ	RC20		ASSTD	1.32	22.44
20-7/12	DZ	RD21		ASSTD	1.50	30.88
3-5/6	DZ	RE20		ASSTD	1.90	6.90
(none)	DZ	RE21		ASSTD		
1	DZ	RF 20		ASSTD	2.40	2.40
1	DZ	RF21		ASSTD	2.40	2.40
4½	DZ	RH21		ASSTD	3.60	16.20
17-2/3	DZ	RI20		ASSTD	4.80	84.80
6-5/6	DZ	RJ20			6.00	41.00
						232.22

Howard — Do not enter this on the payables Rumrill made arrangements with

Each Box contained 1 Doz. No box contained more than one shape

POSITIVELY NO ALLOWANCE FOR BREAKAGE IN TRANSPORTATION

Gonder writes a note to Howard Kline (bookkeeper), saying, "Howard — Do not enter this on the payables Rumrill made arrangements with."

Arkansas, and was manufactured in Ohio at the Florence Pottery Company.

In May of 1939, Gonder and the Florence Pottery Company, on behalf of George Rumrill, acquired the rest of the RumRill inventory that was made at Shawnee.

RumRill pottery continued to be produced in Mt. Gilead, Ohio, from January 1939 all the way up to the fire that occurred on October 16, 1941. The fire destroyed the whole plant and it was claimed as an entire loss. The Florence Pottery Company did not have funds to rebuild. Shortly after that, Rumrill was diagnosed with tuberculosis and the end was imminent.

Many of the molds were salvaged from the fire, and were taken to nearby Zane Pottery Company so that Rumrill could regroup and continue producing pottery.

Within six weeks after the fire, Gonder secured financial backing by attorney Charles McGreevey so that he could start his own pottery company, Gonder Ceramic Arts. On December 8, 1941, Gonder signed the deed for the former Zane Pottery Company and began his own pottery line – a dream that he had had his entire life and one that could now be lived out.

Gonder's new company afforded RumRill a new home for future production. RumRill pottery continued to be manufactured at Gonder Ceramic Arts Company of Zanesville, Ohio, for nearly a year after the big fire at Florence. Salesmen were armed with their new 1942 RumRill catalog, and advertising was in place. The pottery continued to be sold and it was business as usual.

Shortly after April, Rumrill announced his tuberculosis illness. Lawton Gonder was given full control of RumRill pottery, according to Katherine Kline, wife of Howard Kline, secretary/treasurer of the Florence Pottery Company. "Lawton was in charge of everything."

Production of RumRill pottery at the Gonder facility was phased out when the RumRill Pottery Company decided to close its doors in December of 1942 due to losses associated with the fire and the failing health of George Rumrill.

In one press release dated January 1943, Gonder Ceramic Arts, Inc. announced it had ceased doing a specialized mold business with a "prominent pottery company," however, it never mentions RumRill Pottery. David Fisk, RumRill's top salesman, along with the owner of the Fisk & Fisk Company of New York, later went on to represent Gonder's new line of pottery.

In February 1943, a small press release was issued by the RumRill Pottery Company, published in the *Crockery and Glass Journal*. The press release stated, "the firm has ceased operations due to the illness of George D. Rumrill."

In the July 1943 issue of the *Crockery Glass and Journal*, the press release stated that George Rumrill died on April 20, 1943, from tuberculosis.

After Rumrill's death the country basically forgot about RumRill pottery altogether. Perhaps the reason why RumRill never gained much popularity over the past 65 years was because nobody ever really knew anything about it. Hopefully, through this book, a resurgence of collector interest will take place now that new information has been released about this fascinating pottery and its brief Ohio production period.

This large J-24 mold was on display at a RumRill pottery exhibition held in Mt. Gilead, Ohio.

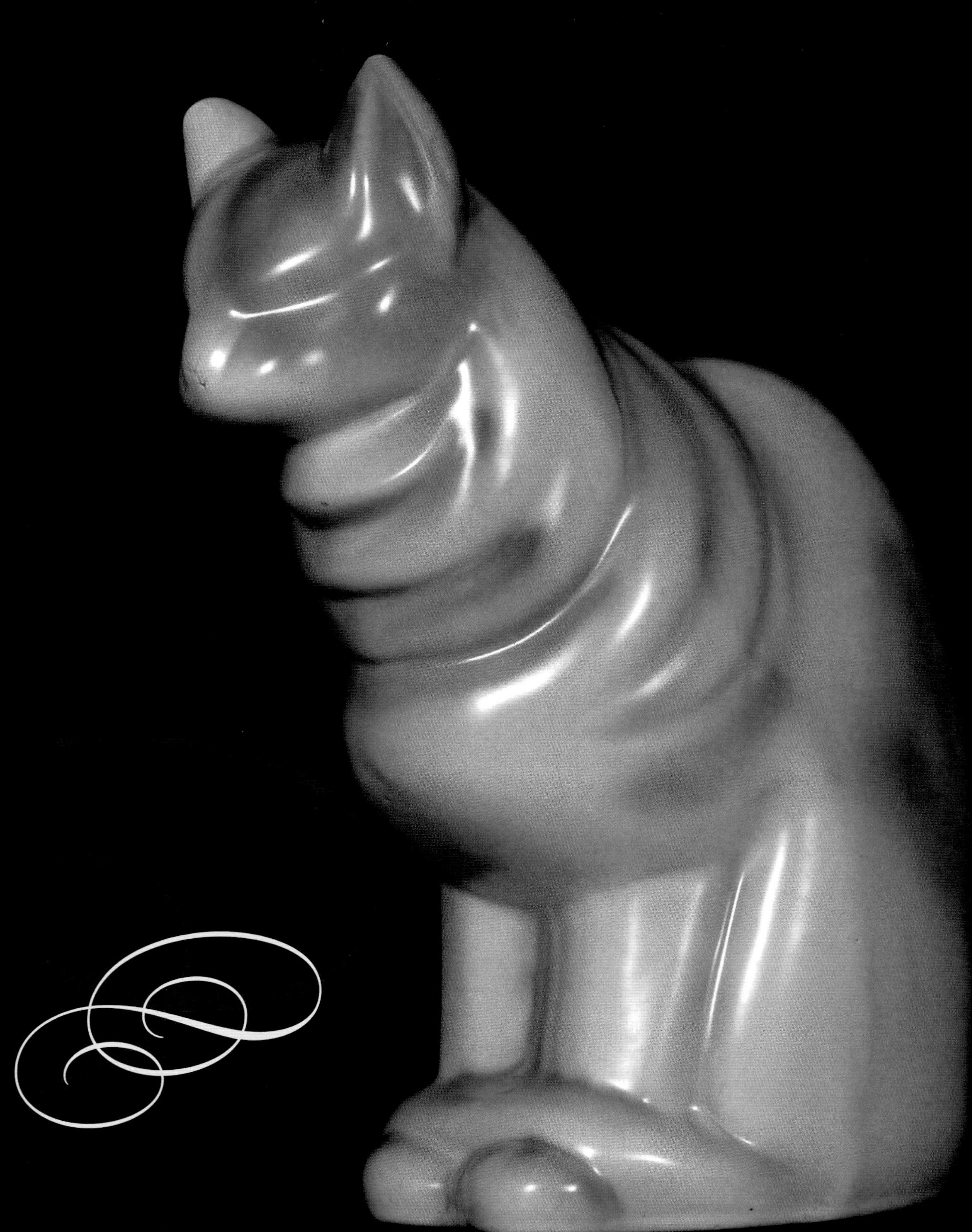

People Who Worked at Florence Pottery Co. and RumRill Pottery

Over 150 people were employed at the Florence Pottery Company in Mt. Gilead, Ohio, during the time that RumRill Pottery was produced there, from 1938 to 1941.

Lawton Gonder was the general business manager of the Florence Pottery Company. He oversaw the operations of RumRill Pottery while it was made there from 1938 to1941. Gonder later went on to start his own company after the Florence Pottery Company burned down in 1941. He continued to manufacture RumRill pottery at his Gonder Ceramic Arts Company in Zanesville, Ohio, but production of RumRIll pottery at that facility was phased out when George Rumrill decided to close its doors in December of 1942. RumRill Pottery ceased operations and David Fisk later went on to represent Gonder's own line of pottery.

Howard Kline was the bookkeeper for Florence Potteries. Kline also held the position of secretary/treasurer and was supposedly on the board of directors at the Florence Pottery Company.

Howard Kline at the time he worked for the Florence Pottery Company.

Wallace Dale McLain was a factory worker at the Florence Pottery Company. He was a spray painter and was responsible for "patenting" the Forest Fire glaze which was the yellow, orange, brown, and sometimes red finish.

Eileen Rultnik was a factory worker at the Florence Pottery Company in Mt. Gilead, Ohio.

Chet Howard was in charge of the kiln.

Ileen Carmean worked for Florence Pottery from 1938 to 1940. She worked in the stockroom.

Helen Hershner also worked in the stockroom at the Florence Pottery Company, from 1936 through 1940. Her main responsibility was a "finisher." According to an article that appeared in the *Marion Star* on January 4, 1981, "when objects came out of the molds they were very fragile, she said, and there were ridges where two or more parts of the mold came together. She carefully cut off the ridges with a knife, then washed the places with water to make them smooth. The objects then were put in the kiln."

Louise Bauer was a freelance designer for the RumRill Pottery Company. She designed vases, miniatures, and a dinnerware line called Sherry-Louise, which was named after Rumrill's daughter and herself. Louise also worked for Walt Disney, Shawnee, and Hull.

Louise Bauer in her studio in Zanesville, Ohio. *Crockery and Glass Journal*, January 1941.

People Who Worked at Florence Pottery Co. and RumRill Pottery

Rudy Ganz designed the potters' wheel for Shawnee Pottery and the RumRill Pottery Company.

Evelyn Taylor was the executive secretary at the Florence Pottery Company. She worked for bookkeeper Howard Kline and Lawton Gonder, then general manager.

Charles Bane was the packer and he worked in the shipping department.

Ted Howard and Andy Clark worked in the factory.

Evelyn Taylor and the author, Francesca Fisher.

Woody Harper was the supervisor in the shipping department at Florence Pottery Company.

Virginia Brown worked in the factory.

Andy Wells and his wife worked in the office across the street from the Florence Pottery plant.

Eurich Bruce was a shareholder and the money behind the RumRill Pottery Company's operation at the Florence Pottery Company.

Harold "Dutch" West was a factory worker and the superintendent at the Florence Pottery Company. He was also the foreman of the shipping department.

Harold "Dutch" West with his Modern Cat doorstop.

Hobert Allen Beard worked on the line at the Florence Pottery Company factory.

David Fisk was the sales manager for RumRill Pottery. His territory covered New York and the eastern United States. His company was called Fisk & Fisk, Inc., and it was based in New York City.

C. Q. Robinson was a salesman for RumRill Pottery. His territory covered the west coast.

Harry O. RumRill was a salesman who worked for RumRill Pottery. His territory covered Illinois, Ohio, and Indiana.

Other salesmen included A. C. "Happy" Morris (southwestern U.S.); Hal Copeland (southeastern U.S.); Paul J. Freeman; Mr. Aust; Mr. Glasner; Mr. Scott; and Mr. Nash.

Albert Kessler & Co. distributed RumRill pottery in San Francisco.

R. L. Andrews, who was formerly a salesman for Weller, joined RumRill in 1941. He represented RumRill Pottery in Minnesota, Iowa, Colorado, and parts of Michigan and Wisconsin.

Mildred Edgell and Edith Frances Rumrill (George's sister) worked at the RumRill Pottery Company headquartered in Little Rock, Arkansas.

Surprisingly, the cover of the 1940 catalog shows that even George Rumrill's son, Jack Rumrill, was involved with the company as its assistant sales manager.

Hobert Allen Beard in a photo taken 25 years before he worked at Florence Pottery Company. Photo provided by Barbara Borck, daughter.

George Rumrill was the sales manager for the RumRill Pottery Company of Little Rock, Arkansas.

Pottery maker George Rumrill.

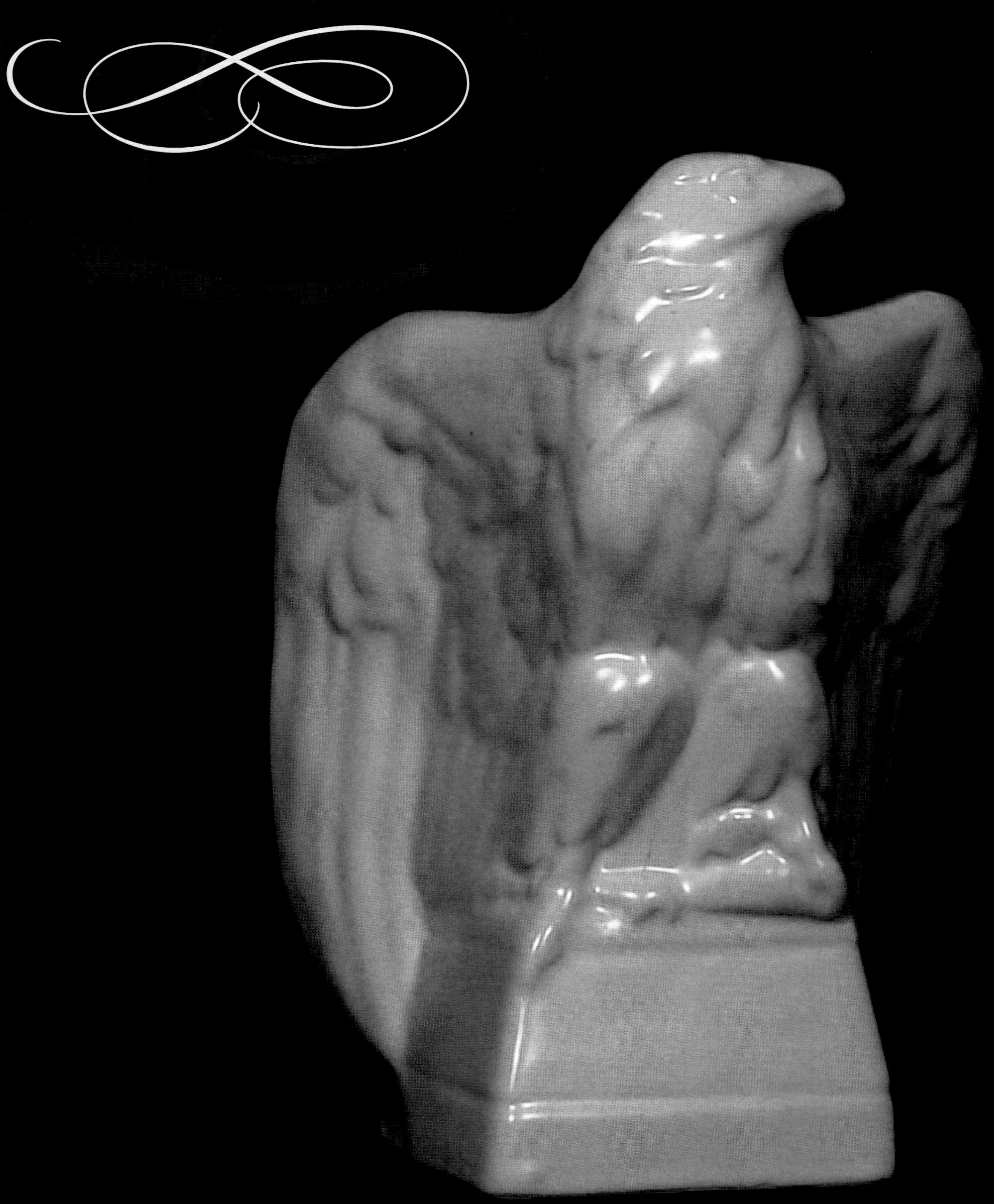

The Molds and Mold Designers

George Rumrill was a pottery visionary. He traveled extensively securing new accounts and, at the same time, attended trade shows in an effort to scope out the competition. He would see something that he liked that was being made by other pottery companies, and would either buy it and send it to Gonder, or he would sketch it and send it him. Gonder would make up a similar object and tweak it just a little bit so that it was different from the competition's.

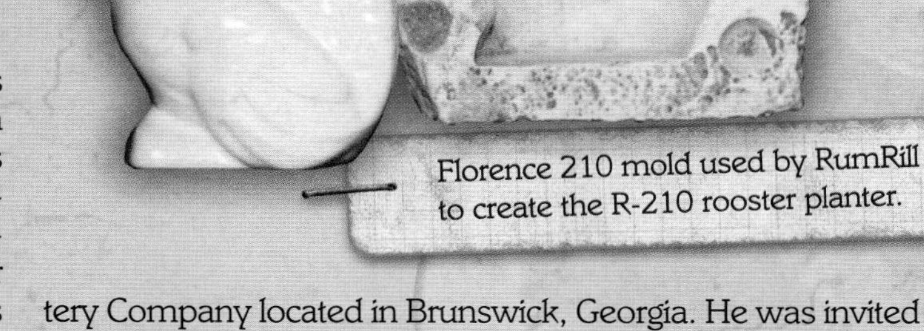

Florence 210 mold used by RumRill to create the R-210 rooster planter.

Prior to Rumrill having his pottery made in Mt. Gilead, his first molds were used by the Shawnee Pottery Company in 1938 and 1939. In an interview I did with Bernard Twiggs back in 1996, he told me that the American Products Company manufactured the molds for the RumRill Pottery Company. Mr. Twiggs also told me that he and George Schworber did the modeling and block and casing based on the designs given to them by George Rumrill. Twiggs and Schworber also worked at the Shawnee Pottery Company.

According to documents on file with the Morrow County Historical Society, in a letter addressed from Lawton Gonder to the Shawnee Pottery Company, it states that the "truck took the last of the molds" which suggests that Florence bought the RumRill molds from Shawnee. Additionally, a bill of record is signed by Addis Hull on May 17, 1939.

The Shawnee molds were reused at Florence Pottery Company when Rumrill started there in 1939. Rumrill also adopted many of Florence's molds and remarketed them under the "RUMRILL" name. Shown above is an example of one of the reused molds from the Florence-RumRill transition.

Paul Herold and Mr. Machet, also known as "the Frenchman," were artists that submitted drawings to either Gonder and/or George Rumrill. Rumrill and Gonder decided which designs would be good sellers, and, if and when accepted, the artists were paid for their services. Miss Wieselthier was another designer that worked for RumRill, and she worked through the summer of 1940.

Rudy Ganz designed the potter's wheel which is known as the RumRill Dealer Sign. RumRill didn't like paying out to "modelers" since their charges were so high.

Alfred Lawton modeled, designed, and offered recommendations of glaze effects for RumRill Pottery in October of 1939. Lawton owned the Englecraft Pottery Company located in Brunswick, Georgia. He was invited by George Rumrill to work with Florence Pottery Company to help design several new and original shapes and finishes.

Louise Bauer designed the Sherry-Louise dinnerware line. Louise was a freelancer and worked for Shawnee, Hull, and Disney, as well as other pottery makers.

Harvey E. Tracey was responsible for the creation and design of the J-20, a patented feeder arm and self-watering flowerpot. Below is the correspondence first dated March 16, 1940, from Harvey Tracey to the Florence Pottery Company regarding the changes required by the patent department in order for the patented feeder arm to get approved. After the fire destroyed the Florence Pottery Plant, Gonder took the J-20 mold with him so that he could manufacture and sell this patented flowerpot through Gonder Ceramic Arts.

The blueprint that was supposedly submitted to the Patent and Trademark Office for the J-20 patented feeder arm. Courtesy Morrow County Historical Society

rumrill
MADE IN U. S. A.

Problems with the Pottery

George Rumrill knew how to be successful in business. He had the winning combination of a great product and consumer demand. He employed all the right people to be part of his team. His aggressive salesmen were able to secure large accounts and orders kept coming in all the time. The RumRill Pottery Company was a regular and monthly advertiser in all the trade journal magazines. Additionally, Rumrill would keep the public apprised of new developments by frequently sending out press releases.

However, just like in any business, the ability to supervise from afar had its disadvantages. He was in Arkansas, and the manufacturing plant was in Ohio. Problems at the plant occurred frequently, which hurt his business immensely. Inasmuch as Rumrill tried to rectify situations by sending letters pointing out these problems, the letters seemed to do no good. The problems kept happening over and over again. Shipments weren't being checked for accuracy and a lot of mistakes happened. There were several instances that the pottery was being made and not even stamped or stickered "RUMRILL."

Miscommunication and lack of supervision was a large part of the problem. Orders weren't being fulfilled in a timely manner, cartons were being packed haphazardly and breakage was occurring, substitutions were being made on shapes and finishes, deadlines were being missed, and seconds were being sold. These nightmare situations thwarted Rumrill's business plans so much that his pottery soon developed a bad reputation among retailers. He lost accounts over these situations, and eventually, nobody wanted to do business with him. Word was out: Rumrill could not deliver what he promised. Even when it was delivered, it arrived broken! These situations were very embarrassing to Rumrill and his salesmen.

To make matters worse, Rumrill changed his mind frequently and was always changing directions. He discontinued shapes, changed finish colors, renamed sizes, and whipped up new ideas virtually overnight. This caused a great deal of confusion at Florence. Nobody seemed to know what they were doing. Catalogs were even mismarked, which caused even more problems for the packers on the other end. In one letter, an entire shipment of E-12's was sent back because the packers sent E-21's instead.

Seconds were being sold on the streets, and when Rumrill caught wind of it, he confronted Gonder about the situation. In a letter dated March 13, 1940, RumRill says, "this item of you selling seconds and not letting us have entire control of our pottery is rapidly coming to a show down." The fights went on and on.

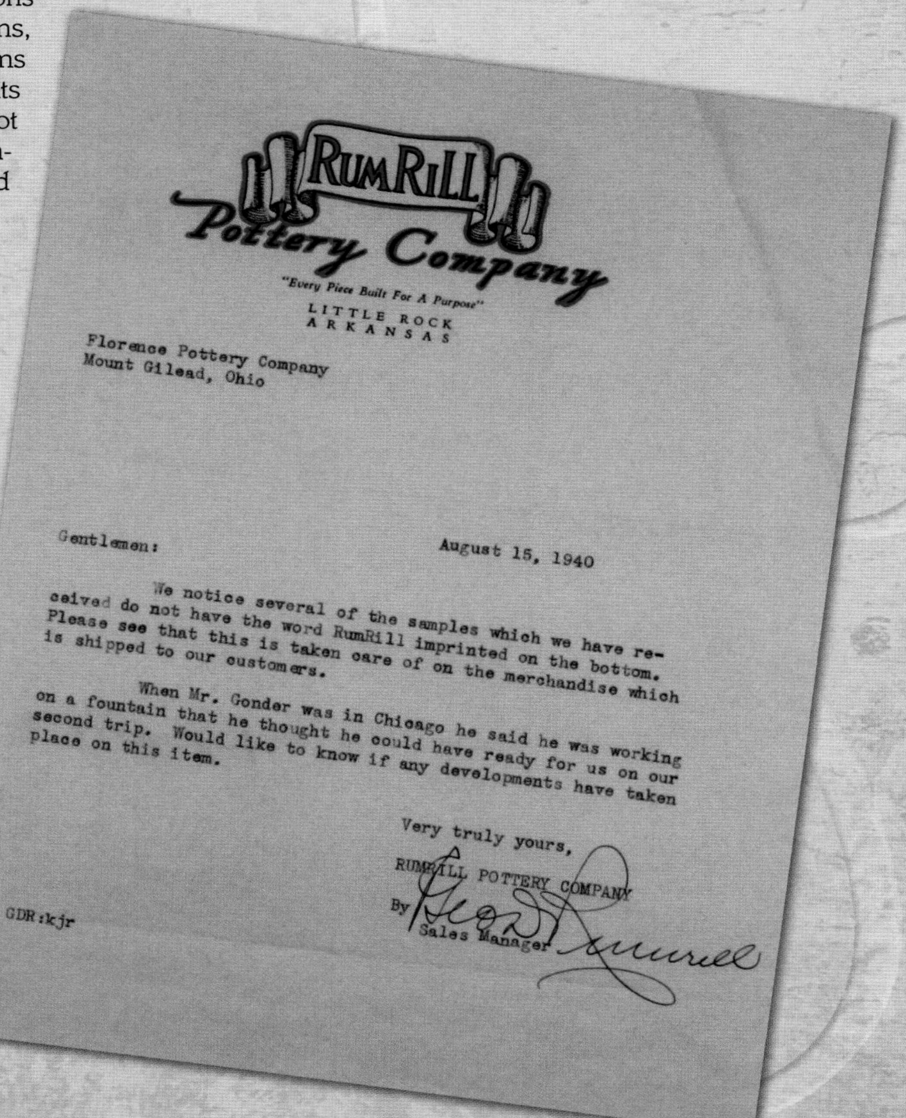

RumRill Pottery Company
"Every Piece Built For A Purpose"
LITTLE ROCK
ARKANSAS

Florence Pottery Company
Mount Gilead, Ohio

Gentlemen: August 15, 1940

We notice several of the samples which we have received do not have the word RumRill imprinted on the bottom. Please see that this is taken care of on the merchandise which is shipped to our customers.

When Mr. Gonder was in Chicago he said he was working on a fountain that he thought he could have ready for us on our second trip. Would like to know if any developments have taken place on this item.

Very truly yours,
RUMRILL POTTERY COMPANY
By Geo. Rumrill
Sales Manager

GDR:kjr

Problems with the Pottery

Florence also did not move at the rate of speed Rumrill wanted, and situations caused delays and problems with vendors. For instance, one of RumRill's accounts wanted a dog dish made for them. Although the order from RumRill's corporate headquarters in Arkansas was very clear in stating the dimensions that the dog dish had to be, the prototype that Florence produced for the customer didn't even come close to what was ordered. As Edith Rumrill described in one of her letters, "the bowl wasn't high enough, and therefore, a cocker spaniel's ears would get in the dish."

Florence had a hard time keeping up with an overly enthusiastic George Rumrill. George wanted things done practically overnight, and Gonder's crew simply could not put it together at the speed Rumrill wanted. Another instance is that Rumrill wanted bowls and specific dinnerware items. Three months had passed and Rumrill still didn't have any samples to show to his customers! These delays cost him business… valuable business.

Erie Dry Goods, one of RumRill's big accounts, would not order from them again after a shipment was unpacked right in front of the salesman, David Fisk. The large M-8 vases were crammed in the carton and hardly any paper was used to securely pack the order. Almost all the candlesticks arrived broken. Erie Dry Goods said the breakage was "excessive." Although a claim was submitted against the railroad company, Erie Dry Goods was still out money because the railroad company only paid a claim by its weight.

Rumrill wanted to stay on the road and sell, sell, sell (which is what he did best), but problems kept happening at the plant and over and over again. Rumrill tried to be as diplomatic as possible in the beginning, but situations weren't being rectified. Rumrill would sometimes write five to six letters a day to Florence, and all he did was complain about the mistakes that were happening. These letters often went ignored! It is hard to fathom how any work could be done because it took so much time to read these long-winded letters, let alone respond to every little detail that was outlined. One can easily construe that it almost seems like some sort of sabotage was happening and that these things were being done intentionally in an effort to put RumRill out of business.

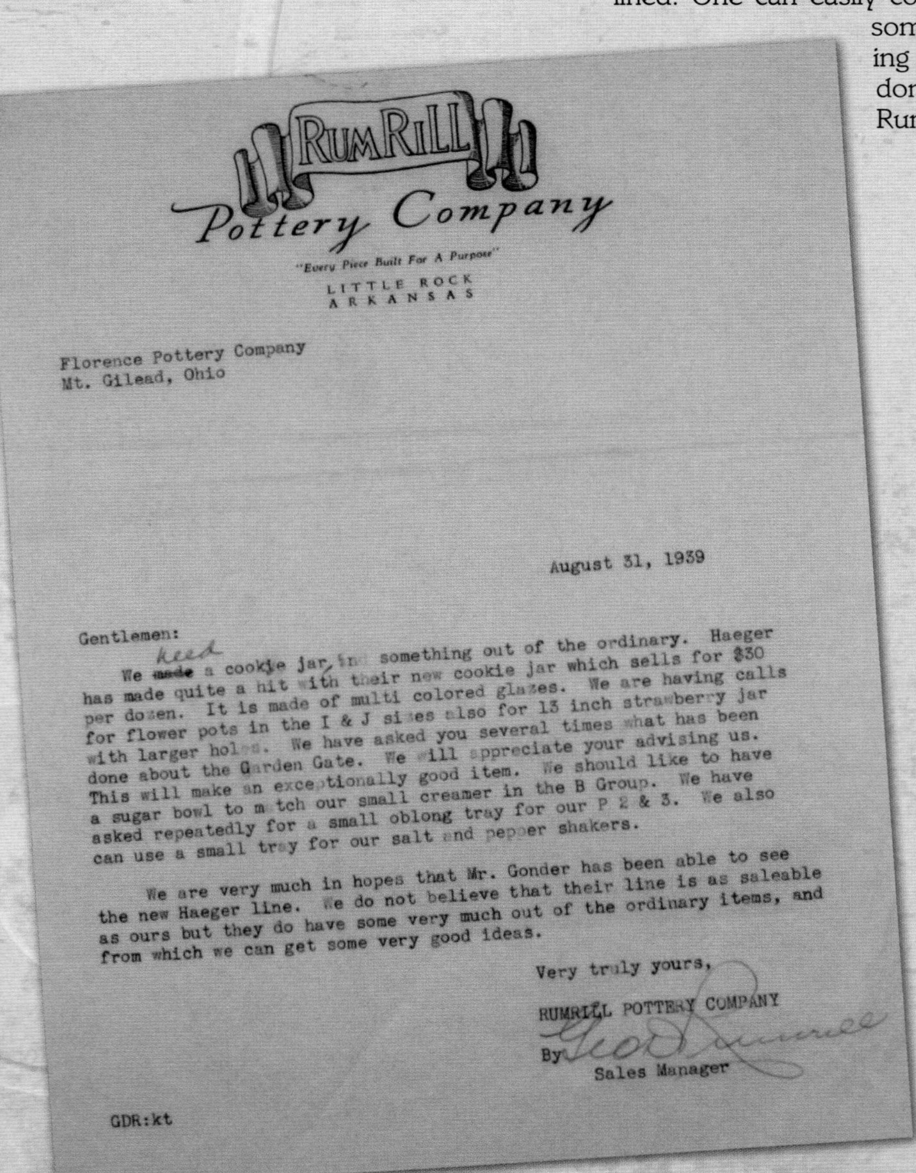

RumRill Pottery Company

"Every Piece Built For A Purpose"

LITTLE ROCK
ARKANSAS

Florence Pottery Company
Mt. Gilead, Ohio

August 31, 1939

Gentlemen:

We ~~made~~ need a cookie jar, in something out of the ordinary. Haeger has made quite a hit with their new cookie jar which sells for $30 per dozen. It is made of multi colored glazes. We are having calls for flower pots in the I & J sizes also for 13 inch strawberry jar with larger holes. We have asked you several times what has been done about the Garden Gate. We will appreciate your advising us. This will make an exceptionally good item. We should like to have a sugar bowl to match our small creamer in the B Group. We have asked repeatedly for a small oblong tray for our P 2 & 3. We also can use a small tray for our salt and pepper shakers.

We are very much in hopes that Mr. Gonder has been able to see the new Haeger line. We do not believe that their line is as saleable as ours but they do have some very much out of the ordinary items, and from which we can get some very good ideas.

Very truly yours,

RUMRILL POTTERY COMPANY

By Geo D Rumrill
Sales Manager

GDR:kt

Each person pointed his or her finger and tried to put the blame on the other fellow. The fights that ensued were almost comical sometimes. Rumrill made an example by saying something to the effect of, "for crying out loud, the customer ordered a C-5 but was sent a B-2. Don't your workers look at the bottom of the piece and compare it to the order form before packing it?"

At one point, things were so totally out of control, Rumrill's sister suggested he pay a personal visit to Florence so that everything could get straightened out. Either Gonder was a terrible manager, or somebody wasn't supervising the crew.

There were also overruns which were made in error, and this caused excess inventory to sit around. Situations like this caused the Florence Pottery Company and the Rum-Rill Pottery Company to lose money. There can be no profit when there are mistakes in business.

At one point, the plant was over-staffed, but the workers sat around with nothing to do because no orders were coming in. Then a rush of orders came in, and everything got back-ordered. Some customers were so tired of waiting for their shipments, they canceled their orders. This usually happened the day after the items were made! Florence would now be stuck with unsold inventory, and Rumrill's customer would not order from him again because the turnaround wasn't quick enough.

All these situations were sources of aggravation for Rumrill. He ran a tight ship back in Arkansas, especially alongside his proficient letter-writing sister. It's no wonder that the poor guy got sick. He had a lot of problems!

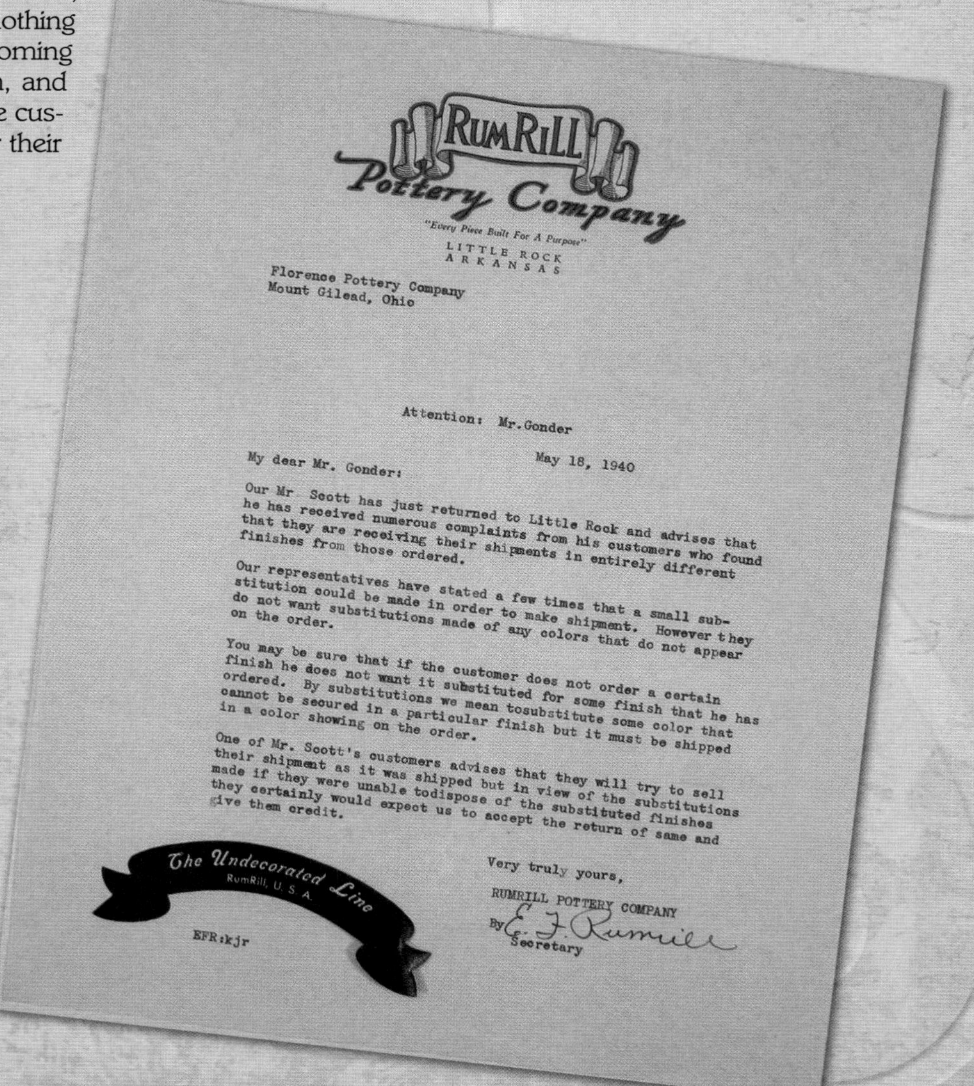

RUMRILL
Pottery Company
"Every Piece Built For A Purpose"
LITTLE ROCK
ARKANSAS

Florence Pottery Company
Mount Gilead, Ohio

Attention: Mr.Gonder

May 18, 1940

My dear Mr. Gonder:

Our Mr Scott has just returned to Little Rock and advises that he has received numerous complaints from his customers who found that they are receiving their shipments in entirely different finishes from those ordered.

Our representatives have stated a few times that a small substitution could be made in order to make shipment. However they do not want substitutions made of any colors that do not appear on the order.

You may be sure that if the customer does not order a certain finish he does not want it substituted for some finish that he has ordered. By substitutions we mean tosubstitute some color that cannot be secured in a particular finish but it must be shipped in a color showing on the order.

One of Mr. Scott's customers advises that they will try to sell their shipment as it was shipped but in view of the substitutions made if they were unable todispose of the substituted finishes they certainly would expect us to accept the return of same and give them credit.

Very truly yours,

RUMRILL POTTERY COMPANY

By E. F. Rumrill
Secretary

EFR:kjr

The Undecorated Line
RumRill, U. S. A.

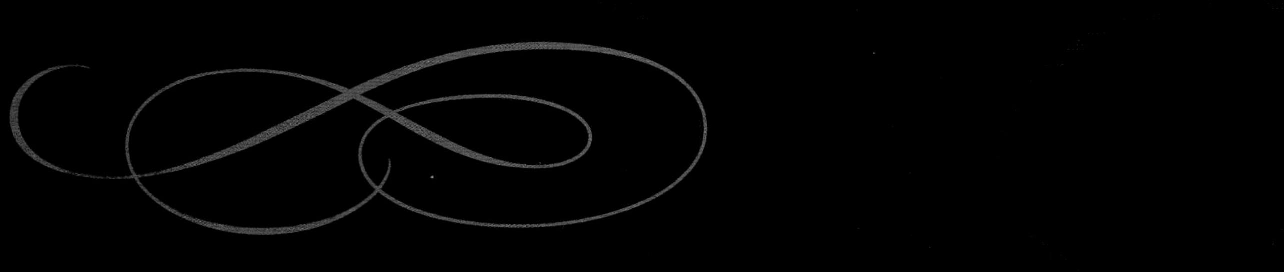

The Mysterious Fire

On October 16, 1941, fire broke out at the Florence Pottery Company, the pottery that made RumRill Pottery. The fire was said to have supposedly started on the second floor. However, there was no electricity or combustibles on the second floor, so arson was suspected. The fire was also confined to a small circular area, which quickly spread due to wood casings and a frame structure. Before long, the entire plant was engulfed in flames.

According to an interview conducted on May 14, 1996, with the former supervisor of the Florence Pottery Company, Harold "Dutch" West, the fire truck showed up at the scene, but the volunteer crew could not figure out how to get the water out of the 1,000-gallon cistern. The situation was hopeless as the whole town watched the factory burn down.

West said his janitors started work at 11 p.m., and at 12:15 a.m. West received a call at home that a fire had started. West rushed to the scene and when he went upstairs, he saw a 20-foot round circle of smoke.

West felt with certainty that the fire was intentionally started. He said the molds were kept far away from where the fire started, and that many were salvaged from the fire and taken to a place in Zanesville.

In an interview conducted on April 26, 1999, with Kathryn Kline, husband of bookkeeper Howard Kline, her recollection of the night of the fire was the big kiln was full of pottery when the blaze started. People were ransacking the place, salvaging as much of the pottery as possible. She recounts, "the fire chief (Harold Johnstone) and his wife gathered up all they could in their arms and ran back and forth from the car to the burning plant. At about her seventh trip to the car, the fire chief's wife found her husband slumped over the car. He had died of a massive heart attack."

The entire plant burned down and the claimed losses were $150,000 – 200,000. On December 4, 1941, an announcement was made that the factory would not be rebuilt.

TO OUR FRIENDS AND CUSTOMERS

We sincerely regret the inconvenience that the fire at our factory has caused you. This fire has prevented shipment of many of your orders.

We very much appreciate the business which you have given us in the past.

RUMRILL POTTERY for 1942 will be on display at all the shows.

Our best wishes for a successful Fall season—and A Merry Christmas and a Happy and Prosperous New Year.

THE RUMRILL POTTERY COMPANY

LITTLE ROCK — *George D. Rumrill—President* — ARKANSAS

RumRill Pottery Marks, 1938 – 1942

George Rumrill produced many beautiful vases, novelty items, and kitchenware for Red Wing Pottery from 1932 to 1938. However, there are collectors that are unaware that another era existed *after* RumRill left Red Wing: RumRill Pottery — the Ohio years.

During the time that RumRill Pottery was produced in Ohio between the years 1938 and 1942, several marks were used to distinguish producers. In fact, these profoundly different marks not only identify the manufacturer, but also the period the piece was produced.

After Rumrill left Red Wing, an alliance took place with the newly formed Shawnee Pottery Company of Zanesville, Ohio. Shawnee could manufacture RumRill pottery at a lower cost, which could be afforded by many people, not just the well-to-do. But this new venture away from Red Wing meant making all new molds and finishes.

According to former Shawnee employees, Rumrill's relationship with Shawnee began as early as April of 1938 and lasted less than a year. One of the problems associated with the breakup was the waterproofing of the vases. It was said that Rumrill left in a fit of rage over this ongoing problem, which was promised to be corrected, but never was.

The most common Shawnee-made RumRill mark consists of the RumRill signature in lowercase, roman-style letters, "rumrill," with a thick line above and below the name. This mark can be impressed or raised on a block and a shape number consisting of a letter and number will usually accompany it.

The large, stamped RumRill mark could not fit on the smaller vases, so the designers adopted a smaller, recognizable mark which consisted of a lowercase double-r mark with one of the r's reversed. This mark was used at the Shawnee Pottery Company for less than a year during 1938. Sometimes a hyphen was used to separate the lowercase r's, and sometimes the rr's will be facing in the same direction. I do not own a piece that is marked this way, but other collectors have reported that some of their pots are marked this way.

Another mark was also used on the Shawnee-made RumRills. These pieces are highly distinguishable from the Florence-made RumRills as they have an "R" in front of the shape number, i.e., RA, RB, RC, RD, etc. These early Shawnee-made pieces were sold for less than a year. The "R" was later dropped so that pottery items made by the Florence Pottery Company would have just one shape letter and number. To see all the shapes offered in 1938, see the 1938 RumRill catalog in the Catalogs chapter.

An RH-9 vase with the stamped Shawnee RumRill marking on the bottom.

RumRill Pottery Marks, 1938 – 1942

When he left Shawnee, George Rumrill found another home at the Florence Pottery Company in Mt. Gilead, Ohio. RumRill pottery was manufactured at the Florence Pottery Company from 1939 until the plant burned down in October of 1941. A variety of bottom markings were used during this time.

One of the many marks used at the Florence Pottery Company, 1939 – 1942.

In 1941, Rumrill was forced to mark his vases with a "MADE IN U.S.A." mark on the bottom of each vase. Documents and letters provided by the Morrow County Historical Society showed that shipments to Canada were refused based on the vases not showing a source of origin. This was not only a costly mistake for RumRill Pottery, but the inventory on hand had to be remarked so that it could be exported to Canada. Canada would not accept the stickers that said "MADE IN USA." Pieces had to be kiln-fired with the imprint.

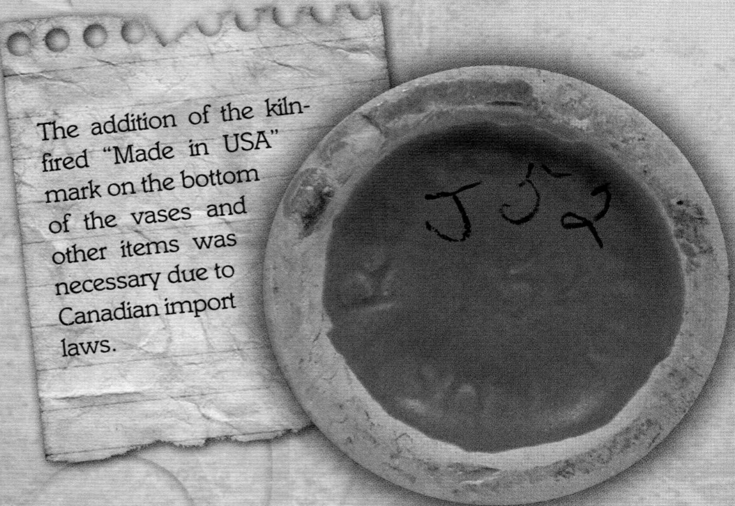

The addition of the kiln-fired "Made in USA" mark on the bottom of the vases and other items was necessary due to Canadian import laws.

A variety of marks were used when Rumrill began to import his wares. Some are marked with "MADE IN USA" on the outer bottom edge of the piece. Some are just marked with "RUMRILL," the shape number, and the letters "USA" on the bottom. Some are also marked with periods in the "U.S.A."

In 1942, Rumrill began stylizing the mark. The R's in the RumRill mark show the flamboyant tails like the L's in RumRill. This mark is often found on pieces produced later on and towards the end of the era.

Pieces marked like this are usually heavier in weight and have a dry edge around a semi-glazed bottom.

During 1942, the attention seemed to focus more on glazes and shapes. Large, abstract-designed pieces and Gothic shapes replaced the Deco and Nouveau styles that had been previously produced from 1938 to 1941. Experimental finishes were used on many of these pieces, particularly the larger Classics Line, consisting of a 16" shell bowl, the large fish statue, and other sea life shapes. They were finished in soft muted shades of green and tan, and their interiors were usually a high gloss pink finish. These large pieces also had

Rare ash black bottoms had a distinctive reverse impressed mark. These pieces were made during the transition period when Gonder started producing Rumrill Pottery, and after George Rumrill announced his illness. Note how the letters are set in reverse.

Another unusual marking was found on the bottom of this F-28 vase. The "USA" is reversed.

an unusual a charcoal black bottom — another sign of a Gonder-made RumRill. These unglazed bottoms were also sometimes numbered with a three-digit shape number, starting with the 500 series. These pieces were produced in late 1941 and 1942 at the Zane Pottery Company which later was renamed Gonder Ceramic Arts.

Press releases were still being printed about RumRill Pottery's new lines, and it continued to be made at Gonder Ceramic Arts through 1942. During that time, Rumrill announced that he had tuberculosis and his health began to fail. He could no longer oversee the operations of his products. Lawton Gonder was given full control by George Rumrill.

Towards the very end of RumRill production, several pieces were made by Gonder that bear the RumRill mark. These pieces are glazed to look exactly like Gonder pottery; however, they are marked "RUMRILL." Most of them can be found in a highly glazed gray finish accompanied by a high gloss pink interior. The only way to tell them apart is by flipping them over and looking at how they are marked. These RumRill pieces are quite scarce.

In 1943, Gonder reused some of the molds from the RumRill pottery line and Florence Pottery Company to produce his own line of pottery, Gonder Ceramic Arts. Mold swapping was a common practice in the ceramics industry. Always be sure to look at the bottom of a vase before passing it by. You never know… it just might be marked "RUMRILL."

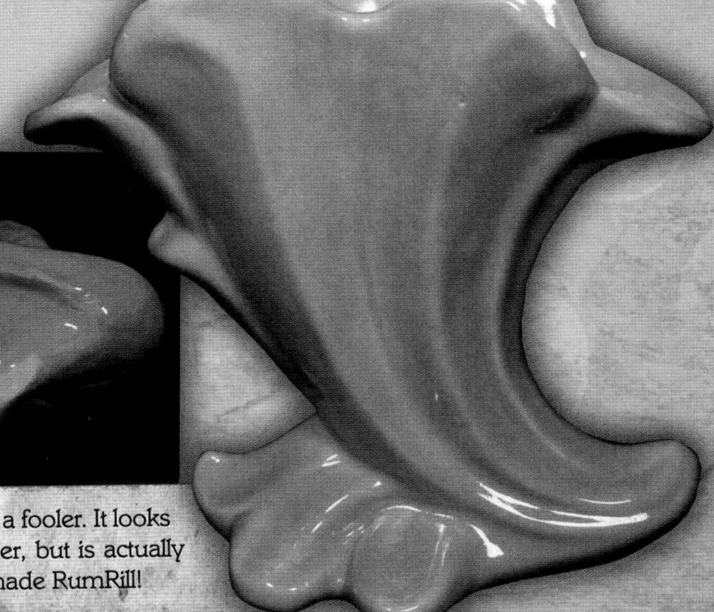

This Gonder-made RumRill mark can be found on the underside of this J-61 vase, manufactured in late 1942. Note the bottom is still marked "RUMRILL," but the glaze is definitely a well-known Gonder finish.

This vase is a fooler. It looks like a Gonder, but is actually a Gonder-made RumRill!

The Finishes and Glazes

The information contained in this section was obtained from historical documents, company catalogs, and interviews conducted with pottery workers at the factories.

It is documented that there were 17 finishes used on the bisque pieces that were made in Ohio from 1938 to 1942. The finish can pinpoint the exact year that any Ohio piece was made. For instance, a popular finish, Gentian Blue, was a deep matte blue color that appears in documents as early as 1938 through April of 1940.

It is obvious that finishes were a big thing as was evidenced through letters written back and forth by George Rumrill and Lawton Gonder. If the pottery was a good seller, it either meant there was a need for that shape, or the color was popular with buyers.

One of George Rumrill's chief responsibilities included attending as many trade shows as possible. He would act as a corporate spy, so to speak, and he would see what the competition was doing. He would take notes and report back to Gonder any new colors or "spray" he would see while he was at the ceramic shows. The events would be memorialized and Rumrill would sometimes write three or four letters a day on hotel stationery. Rumrill was a proficient note-keeper, and thankfully, through the documentation preserved by several historians, we have proof of this.

Florence Pottery Company was producing flowerpots, planters, and vases in the following finishes in 1937: Eggshell, Aqua, Blue, Yellow, and Rose. Rumrill wanted the same colors used on his pieces as were used at Shawnee. This offered the Florence Pottery Company the opportunity to learn how to mix the different mineral oxides such as tin, iron, zinc, lead, and others in order to create the new color finishes.

Before Rumrill decided to manufacture his pottery at the Florence Pottery Company, he was already using seven different finishes at the Shawnee Pottery Company. According to the 1938 catalog, these finishes included:

1938

No. 1 Parisian White
No. 2 Gentian Blue
No. 3 Sea Spray Green
No. 4 Pheasant Red
No. 5 Parisian White Antiqued
No. 6 Cadet Blue
No. 7 Daffodil Yellow

Blue Stipple, which was very similar to Red Wing's Dutch Blue, was a deep matte blue finish with spongy gray markings. It was produced in very limited quantities in 1938 by the Shawnee Pottery Company for George Rumrill. Pieces that were made in this finish are very hard to find. There is no documentation regarding the name of this finish. Pieces in this finish will be referred to in this book as "Stipple Blue."

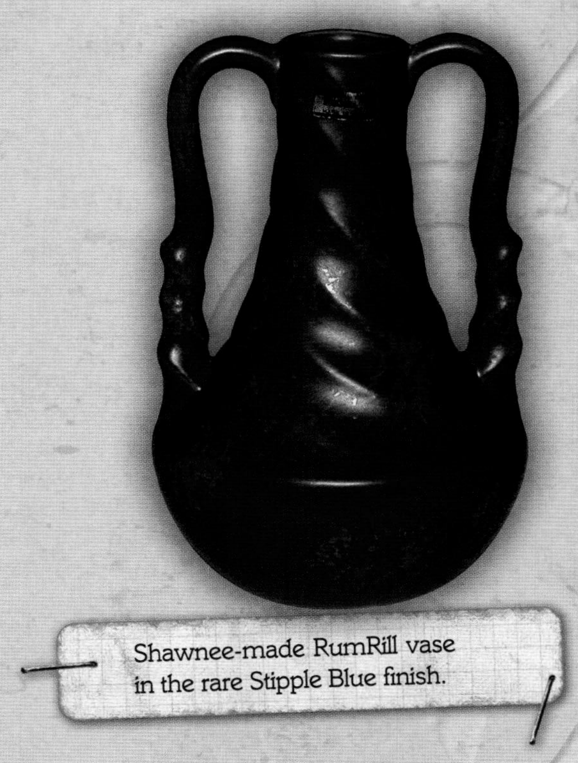

Shawnee-made RumRill vase in the rare Stipple Blue finish.

Mandarin Blue was a highly glazed (shiny) deep blue finish. It does not appear as an available finish in the 1941 catalog, although the Beverage Set continued to be made in this finish as documented by the Summer Promotion literature. There was also another blue called Cadet Blue. This soft pastel light blue finish was used throughout the time RumRill was made in Ohio and at all three manufacturing plants.

Sea Spray Green was another finish that was also used throughout the entire time RumRill Pottery was made in Ohio. The Shawnee-made RumRills in this finish are easy to identify just by their color. The Shawnee Sea Spray Green is so green, it almost looks chartreuse standing next to the Florence Sea Spray Green. All the Shawnee matte finishes are very flat looking in appearance, whereas the Florence-made RumRills have a slight eggshell sheen.

The Finishes and Glazes

Two RumRill vases in the Sea Spray Green finish. The vase on the left was made at Shawnee. The one on the right was made at the Florence Pottery Company. Note the color difference.

In a letter to Rumrill written by Gonder on April 14, 1939, Gonder states that "the red has been materially improved, but we still are not satisfied with it." In this same letter, Gonder asks Rumrill what he thinks about "an overspray on the white for the tenth color." It is this writer's belief that the finish discussed in this letter later became known as Ashes of Roses, a finish that was used for less than one year.

As you have seen in the photos of the Collection in the front of the book, some of the reds that were used as finishes include the Shawnee-made Pheasant Red, then the Florence-made Dubonnet, Burgundy Red, and Ashes of Roses. Each finish is distinctly different.

It is the author's opinion that the finish called Dubonnet is the softer, more mauve-looking red, whereas Burgundy Red is the highly glazed, oxblood-looking red.

RumRill pieces made in the various red colors produced by different pottery companies from 1938 – 1942.

Forest Fire and Forest Green were introduced in 1939. These two finishes later became the "signature finishes" for RumRill pottery, as no other pottery manufacturer used these combination matte finishes on their wares. Even unmarked RumRill pottery is easy to identify by its distinctive colorization and hand-applied finish.

Forest Fire was a beautiful finish of blended yellow, orange, and brown. Red was sometimes used as an accent color. The hand-applied finish gave each piece its own unique look and no two pieces were identical in appearance.

Another hand-applied finish, Forest Green, was an artful combination of green and brown mottling. Sometimes, a bit of gold was added to give it an even more illustrious look.

The Forest Fire and Forest Green finishes were very short lived. Pieces made with these finishes were produced in 1939 and lasted through 1940. Dale McClain, the employee who was the spray painter responsible for these finishes, left Florence Pottery in late 1940 to pursue another job.

According to a newspaper article written on January 4, 1981, by Stark Beard, a *Star Newspaper* reporter, Dale McClain's wife was interviewed and a brief synopsis was given as to how these two finishes were made. "A horizontal green band was spray painted around the object and a dark band was blended in just above the green. Next, vertical flame-colored streaks were painted up from the dark band, giving the illusion of a forest on fire," she states.

In August of 1939, the Modern Line catalog was printed. This catalog "contained 50 new shapes and several new finishes," as announced by George Rumrill in a letter written on January 26, 1940. The finishes were available on the Modern Cat, the Cylindrical Vase, the Modern Ashtrays, and other Art Deco shaped pieces. Note that finishes No. 4 and No. 8 are added to the lineup (Forest Fire and

Forest Green). This was the first time these hand-applied oversprays were used on the pieces. The finishes in the 1939 catalog include:

1939

No. 1 White
No. 2 Gentian Blue
No. 3 Sea Spray Green
No. 4 Forest Fire
No. 5 Mandarin Blue
No. 6 Cadet Blue
No. 7 Daffodil Yellow
No. 8 Forest Green
No. 9 Ashes of Roses

1940

No. 1 Parisian White
No. 2 Gentian Blue
No. 3 Sea Spray Green
No. 4 Forest Fire
No. 5 Mandarin Blue
No. 6 Cadet Blue
No. 7 Buttercup Yellow
No. 8 Forest Green
No. 9 Dubonnet

In August of 1940, it is this writer's belief that, through documentation and letters written by George Rumrill and Lawton Gonder, the finishes at left were used for that year. We know that Gentian Blue was still being used and ordered on goods through April of 1940. The new Hurricane Jug Lamp was also introduced that year, and an advertising pamphlet stated that the finishes shown here were available.

In a letter written later that year on October 4, 1939, Gonder reports to Rumrill and states that "the deep blue matt, the yellow matt, the Forest Fire, and the Mandarin Blue are the lowest production colors." Having this information on hand, RumRill was able to decide what finishes to discontinue and/or replace.

However, it seems that later on in 1940, perhaps towards the latter half of the year, some finishes were dropped, as finishes No. 2 and No. 7 were no longer being offered.

late 1940

No. 1 Parisian White
No. 3 Sea Spray Green
No. 4 Forest Fire
No. 5 Mandarin Blue
No. 6 Cadet Blue
No. 8 Forest Green
No. 9 Ashes of Roses
No. 10 Cameo
No. 11 Apple Blossom

Documentation and sales literature suggests that, since a tenth color was offered, we can surmise that this came right after the 1939 catalog. In a sales bulletin dated December 22, 1939, Rumrill announces his 1940 colors, shown here. He also explains the use of the term "Cameo."

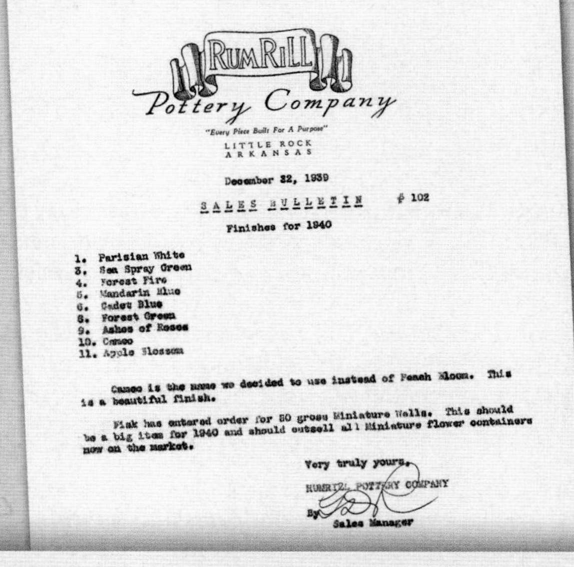

RumRill Pottery Company
"Every Piece Built For A Purpose"
LITTLE ROCK
ARKANSAS

December 22, 1939

SALES BULLETIN # 102

Finishes for 1940

1. Parisian White
3. Sea Spray Green
4. Forest Fire
5. Mandarin Blue
6. Cadet Blue
8. Forest Green
9. Ashes of Roses
10. Cameo
11. Apple Blossom

Cameo is the name we decided to use instead of Peach Bloom. This is a beautiful finish.

Fisk has entered order for 50 gross Miniature Wells. This should be a big item for 1940 and should outsell all Miniature flower containers now on the market.

Very truly yours,
RUMRILL POTTERY COMPANY
By
Sales Manager

Cameo is the name we decided to use instead of Peach Bloom. This is a beautiful finish.

October 4, 1939

George D. Rumrill
Rumrill Pottery Company
Little Rock, Arkansas

Dear Mr. Rumrill:

It is also thought worthy at this time, that we start giving serious consideration as to which colors will be eliminated when the new finishes are put in the line for next year. In our survey and data collected the deep blue matt, the yellow matt, the forest fire, and the mandarin blue are the lowest production colors. I do not know how you want to arrive at the colors to be discontinued, whether you want to go entirely on this, or if you want to carry a brilliant color to keep the line with a certain amount of "kick", which this mandarin blue does, for purposes only, or if you want to get the consensus of opinion of the men on the road as to what the reaction of their daily contacts are. It is well that we be gathering this data, as the time for the presentation of new finishes and the elimination of others, will soon be with us, and we don't want to be forced to act quickly without tangible and well founded reasons.

LG/eb

The Finishes and Glazes

The finishes on the new order form that Rumrill wanted Florence to use match the ones mentioned in the sales bulletin.

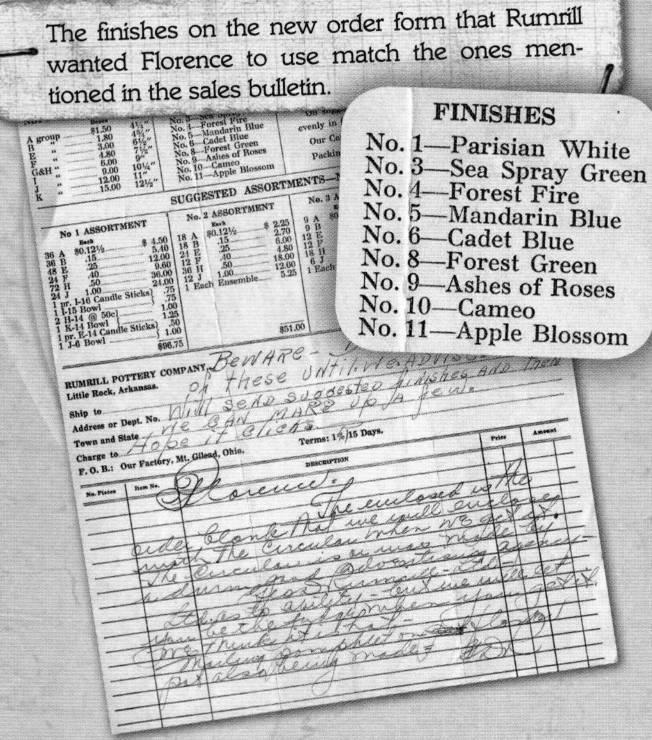

FINISHES

No. 1—Parisian White
No. 3—Sea Spray Green
No. 4—Forest Fire
No. 5—Mandarin Blue
No. 6—Cadet Blue
No. 8—Forest Green
No. 9—Ashes of Roses
No. 10—Cameo
No. 11—Apple Blossom

RUMRILL POTTERY COMPANY, Little Rock, Arkansas.

Terms: 1%/15 Days.

F. O. B.: Our Factory, Mt. Gilead, Ohio.

On December 10, 1940, Lawton Gonder wrote a letter to David Fisk telling him that "the gray is 30% lighter than the sample we sent you and we have eliminated entirely the predominating brown."

1941

No. 1 Parisian White
No. 3 Sea Spray Green
No. 6 Cadet Blue
No. 7 Daffodil Yellow
No. 9 Burgundy Red
No. 10 Cameo
No. 14 Silver Gray

Both Forest Green and Forest Fire finishes do not appear in the first 1941 catalog which lists the finishes shown here. Larger pieces J – X could be ordered in No. 15 White Antique and No. 16 Green Antique.

Silver Gray is perhaps the rarest finish ever used, as it was discontinued during the first quarter of 1941. In a handwritten letter to Gonder from Rumrill (this would have been either written on April 26 or April 27, 1941), he mentions that new catalogs have been printed and that finish No.14 is to be dropped. He also states that "The Staple Line of Pottery" has been added to the brochure, which can be found beneath the potter's wheel on the inside cover. The two inside covers of the 1941 catalogs are shown in the chapter entitled The Catalogs.

By January, 1940, RumRill solidifies his presence in the pottery market and announces in trade journal magazines that he has added "50 new shapes and several new finishes."

In several documents dated August 1940, the new finish No. 10 is referred to as "the sensation of the year." Cameo is the peach color that was used on many pieces produced during that time.

We have concluded that the Cameo finish was used by reviewing a letter written by Edith Rumrill to Lawton Gonder dated November 15, 1940. In this letter, Edith complains that sometimes the Cameo comes out "too pink for her."

Note that finish numbers were reused and reissued. For instance, Parisian White Antiqued is used as Finish No. 5 one year, then Finish No. 5 is referred to as Mandarin Blue shortly thereafter. As mentioned earlier, a lot of mistakes were made when the pottery was packed. The reused finish numbering system probably only added to the confusion of the packers at the factory. There were many instances when orders got messed up and finishes were substituted and, subsequently, the Florence Pottery Company and their crew were blamed for these mistakes. Retailers became very angry when orders arrived that were not packed as specified on the order.

Catalogues are ready and I have asked the office to send you about 10. We are cutting the gray off balance and adding "The staple line of pottery"

late 1941

No. 1 Parisian White
No. 3 Sea Spray Green
No. 6 Cadet Blue
No. 7 Daffodil Yellow
No. 9 Burgundy Red
No. 10 Cameo (Peach)

The finishes used for the latter half of 1941 include those shown here. As in early 1941, larger pieces J – X could be ordered in No. 15 White Antique and No. 16 Green Antique.

Finish No. 17 is mentioned in a letter from George Rumrill to the Florence Pottery Company dated August 19, 1941. Gonder was still experimenting with different glaze treatments and getting them ready for the 1942 catalog.

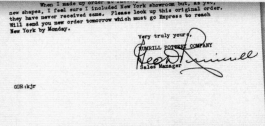

Florence Pottery Company
Mount Gilead, Ohio

When I made up order at factory for # 17 finish and the new shapes, I feel sure I included New York showroom...

When I made up order at factory ... new shapes, I feel sure I included New York showroom but, as yet, they have never received same. Please look up this original order. Will send you new order tomorrow which must go Express to reach New York by Monday.

Very truly yours,
RUMRILL POTTERY COMPANY
Sales Manager

GDR:kjr

The last catalog on record is from 1942 and was used during the time when Gonder was making RumRill pottery at Gonder Ceramic Arts. We know it was printed in 1942 because of a reference to Pearl Harbor.

The Burgundy Red, Cameo, and Green Antique finishes were dropped but were replaced by two new finishes: Two Tone Brown and Neptune Green. Only the B, E, F, G, H, J, K, L, M, and some P items were available that year (the pitcher, cookie jar, and mixing bowls). However, the new Classics Line dominated this catalog and 17 new shapes were introduced that year.

During the last six months of production, the Gonder-produced RumRills incorporated some of Gonder's experimental finishes which included pink interiors and shiny exterior glazes.

These RumRill/Gonder "transitional pieces," as they have become known, are highly distinguishable and easy to identify. They have a distinctive tan and turquoise hand-applied finish with an unglazed black clay bottom. These large oversized pieces include a dolphin vase, a tankard in the shape of a shell, a triple pinecone vase, shell console bowls, large starfish centerpieces, candleholders, and other sea forms. They are marked with a three-digit shape number starting with the number 500, 501, 502, etc. Perhaps the pieces designed and produced at Gonder Ceramic Arts are by far the rarest and most collectible Ohio RumRills.

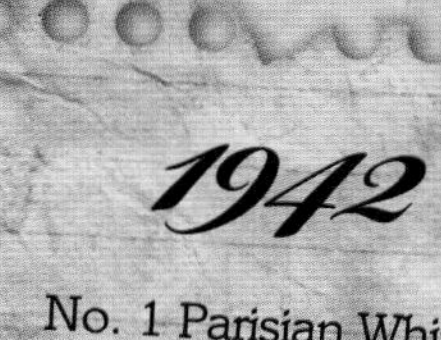

1942

No. 1 Parisian White
No. 3 Sea Spray Green
No. 6 Cadet Blue
No. 7 Daffodil Yellow
No. 15 White Antique
No. 16 Two Tone Brown
No. 17 Neptune Green

The finishes shown here were used in 1942. White Antique and Two Tone Brown were more expensive than the other finishes.

In conclusion, pieces that were made in Mandarin Blue, White Antique, Forest Green, Apple Blossom, Dubonnet, Burgundy Red, Silver Gray, Two Tone Brown, and Neptune Green are the hardest to find and extremely desirable to collectors. These were all short-lived.

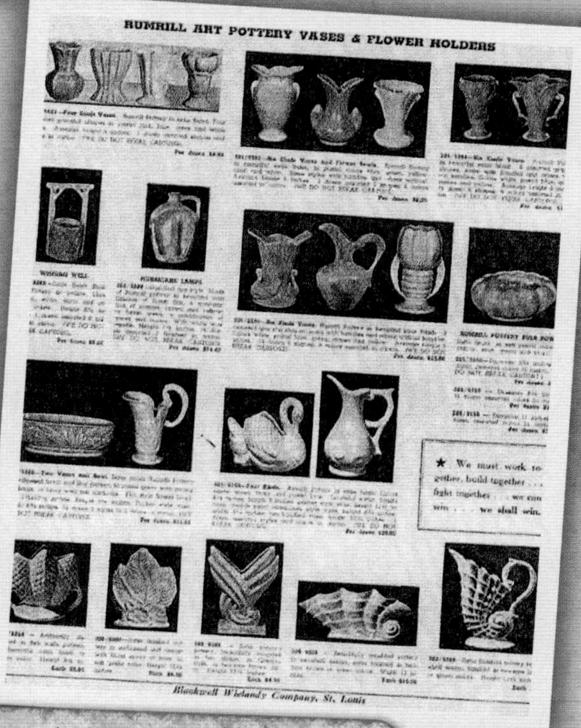

In the last ad on record for RumRill Pottery in 1942, the new Classics Line is advertised by the Blackwell and Wielandy Company of St. Louis, Missouri.

THE STAPLE LINE OF POTTERY

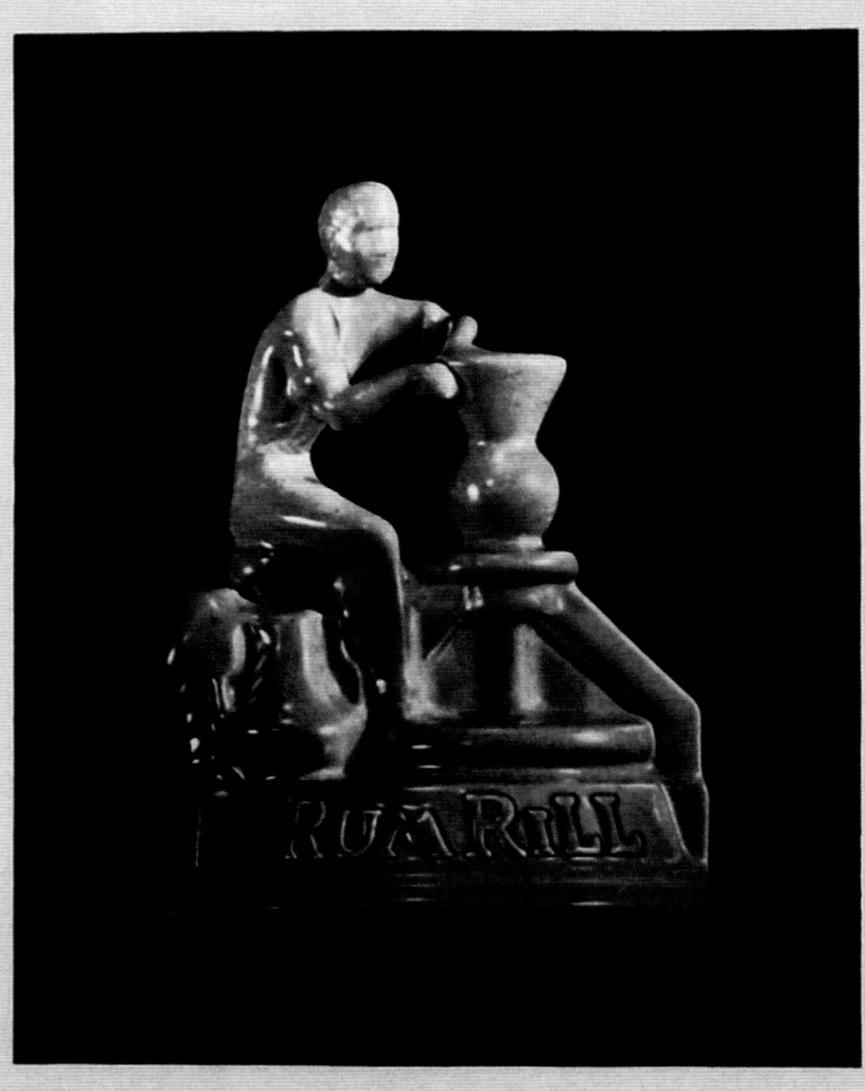

The Catalogs

The following pages are the known catalogs that exist for the RumRill Pottery Company. These catalogs were used from 1938 to 1942. Included is the 1943 –1944 Gonder catalog which shows many of the reused RumRill molds.

The photos below show the 1938 Florence catalog. Many of the shapes were reused and remarketed under the RUMRILL brand.

FLORENCE POTTERY CO.

CRAFTERS OF THE HIGHER TYPE CERAMIC ARTS

Mt. Gilead, Ohio

PHONE NO. 35

The Florence Floral Line

The only quality line manufactured exclusively for Florists.

This new line of florist pottery has a strong sales appeal, and is enabling leading florists to add considerably to their profit column with little sales effort.

Manufactured and sold direct from our factory warehouse in Mt. Gilead, Ohio, at attractive prices. Order your assortment now.

FLORENCE POTTERY CO., MT. GILEAD, OHIO

Group 100—Vases are 4½" high—other pieces in proportion.

Group 200—Vases are 5½" high—other pieces in proportion.
Colors on all items in this line are Eggshell, Aqua, Blue, Yellow, Rose.

FLORENCE POTTERY CO.

Mt. Gilead, Ohio

Vases 20 and 25 are 8½" high—other pieces in proportion.
Colors on all items in this line are Eggshell, Aqua, Blue, Yellow, Rose.

Printed in U. S. A.

1938 Florence catalog.

FLORENCE POTTERY CO.
Mt. Gilead, Ohio

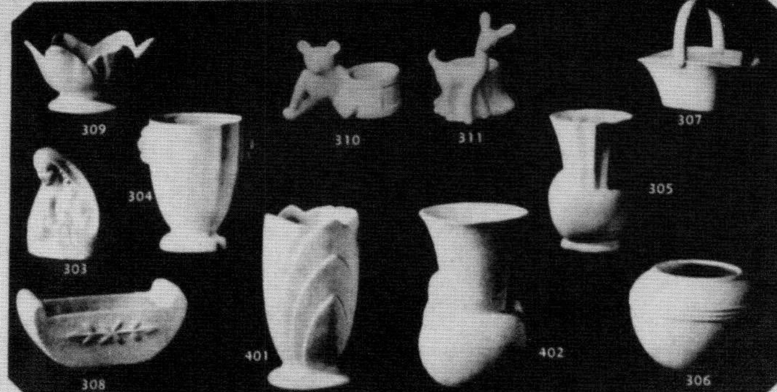

Group 300—Vases are 6" high—other pieces in proportion.
Group 400—Vases are 8" high.

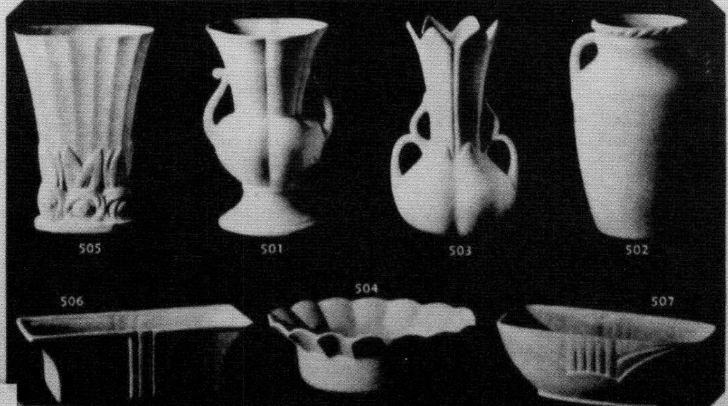

Group 500—Vases are 9¼" high—other pieces in proportion.
Colors on all items in this line are Eggshell, Aqua, Blue, Yellow, Rose.

FLORENCE POTTERY CO.
Mt. Gilead, Ohio

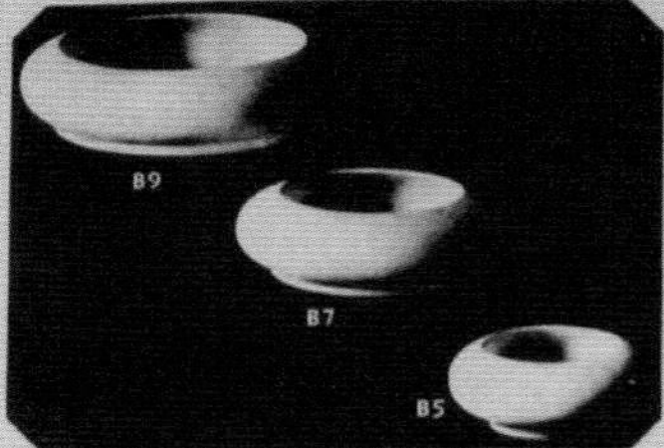

Bulb or Flower Bowls
5"—7"—9" outside diameter

Pots with attached saucers.
3"—4"—5" top diameters.
Same design in Slip Pots in sizes 3" to 8".

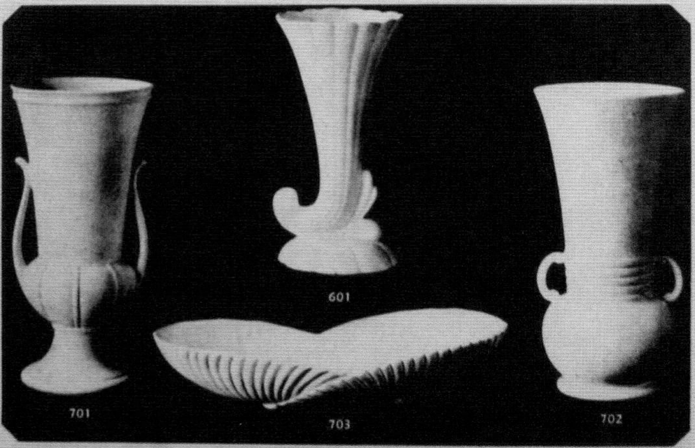

Vase 601—11½" high; Vases 701 and 702, 13½" high; Bowl 703, 15" long.
Colors on all items in this line are Eggshell, Aqua, Blue, Yellow, Rose.
We stock all items in all colors.

1938 Florence catalog.

The following RumRill catalog was used during the time RumRill pottery was made at the Shawnee Pottery Company in 1938.

■ to accomplish this advancement, we transferred our source of supply to zanesville, ohio - - for more than fifty years the country's recognized center of art pottery. here in the very heart of a community of skilled pottery craftsmen . . among men who inherited their art from their fathers, we found the largest and best equipped manufacturer who combined this ability with superior methods of production and produced for us the finest lines in our history ■

illustrated on the following pages are the new rumrill lines of art and specialty pottery for 1938. also listed are the attractive prices, terms and freight rates and a new conception of merchandising in the pottery industry ■ ever since our first year in business, our production volume has constantly increased. we believe this steady growth has been built by strict adherence to a sales policy based on sound business. this policy insists upon . . established price values . . artistically and practically shaped articles . . colors and finishes in tune with the mode-creative-advanced and popular . . products of highest quality which can be produced only by the better materials shaped by the skilled hands of master pottery craftsmen . . prompt service and attention to details . . and sales plans that assist our customers in building bigger profits through increased volume and faster turnover ■ late in 1937 it became increasingly apparent that the continuance of this policy demanded the creation of many new numbers. the modern colors obtained from the newest discoveries and developments in ceramic materials must be included - - more modern and efficient production methods must be utilized to assure you this quality at a price and size which gives you a sales advantage in retailing ■ to accomplish this advancement, we transferred our source of supply to zanesville, ohio - - for more than fifty years the country's recognized center of art pottery. here in the very heart of a community of skilled pottery craftsmen . . among men who inherited their art from their fathers, we found the largest and best equipped manufacturer who combined this ability with superior methods of production and produced for us the finest lines in our history ■ the recently discovered materials demand a secret process of manufacture and represent the latest achievements in ceramic engineering. they produce a pure white body, which when fired to exact temperatures, are more durable than ordinary earthenwares. our glazes in both matt and bright glazes, are beautiful tones of popular colors. they are so compounded and fired that crazing and checking are practically eliminated. both ink and pencil marks can be easily removed from our matt glazes with a damp cloth, and each piece will pass this rigid test ■ as a result of these outstanding improvements, it has been necessary to install additional equipment to meet our requirements. to complete this plan of individualized sales-service we now offer "private brand" merchandise, on orders totalling more than $250. we will affix your own labels at no increase in price. ■ study this plan carefully and compare it with any other from the standpoint of quality, design, and profit to you. then place your order today. use the order blank in the back of this catalog.

RumRill Pottery Company • Little Rock, Arkansas.

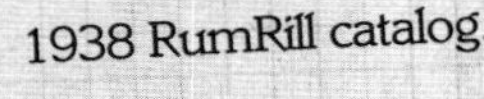

1938 RumRill catalog.

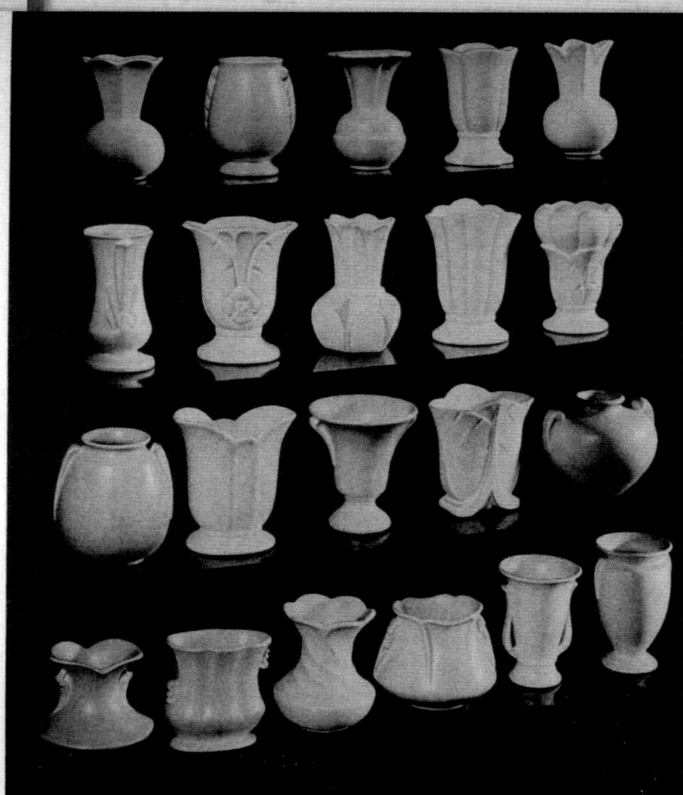

Top Row - Group A - *Left to Right* - RA-3, RA-5, RA-1, RA-6, RA-2

Second Row - Group B - *Left to Right* - RB-2, RB-3, RB-6, RB-4, RB-5

Third Row - Group C - *Left to Right* - RC-4, RC-9, RC-3, RC-10, RC-1

Fourth Row - Group C and D - *Left to Right* - RC-2, RC-7, RC-8, RC-5, RD-2, RD-1

RumRill Pottery Company • Little Rock, Arkansas

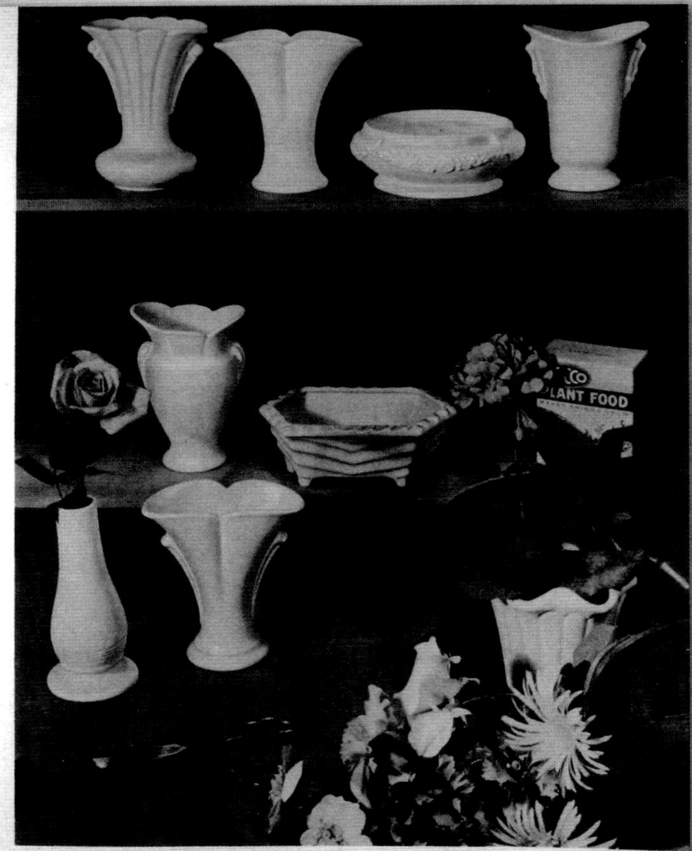

PLANT FOOD
Top Row - Group E - Left to Right - RE-2, RE-11, RE-10, RE-3
Second Row - Group E - Left to Right - RE-1, RE-6
Third Row - Group E - Left to Right - RE-8, RE-4, RE-9
RumRill Pottery Company • Little Rock, Arkansas

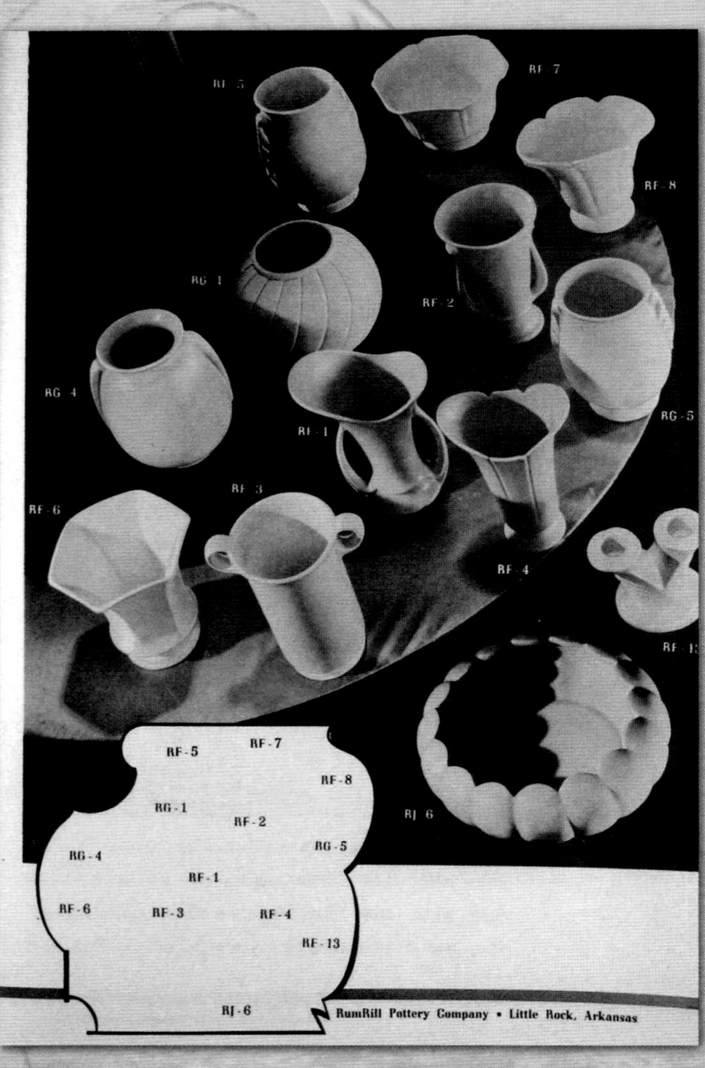

1938 RumRill catalog.

Top Row - Group H - Left to Right - RH-5, RH-13, RH-14, RH-9, RH-7
Second Row - Group H - Left to Right - RH-11, RH-1, RH-3, RH-6
Third Row - Group H - Left to Right - RH-2, RH-12, RH-10, RH-17
Fourth Row - Group H - Left to Right - RH-4, RH-18, RH-15, RH-8, RH-16
RumRill Pottery Company • Little Rock, Arkansas

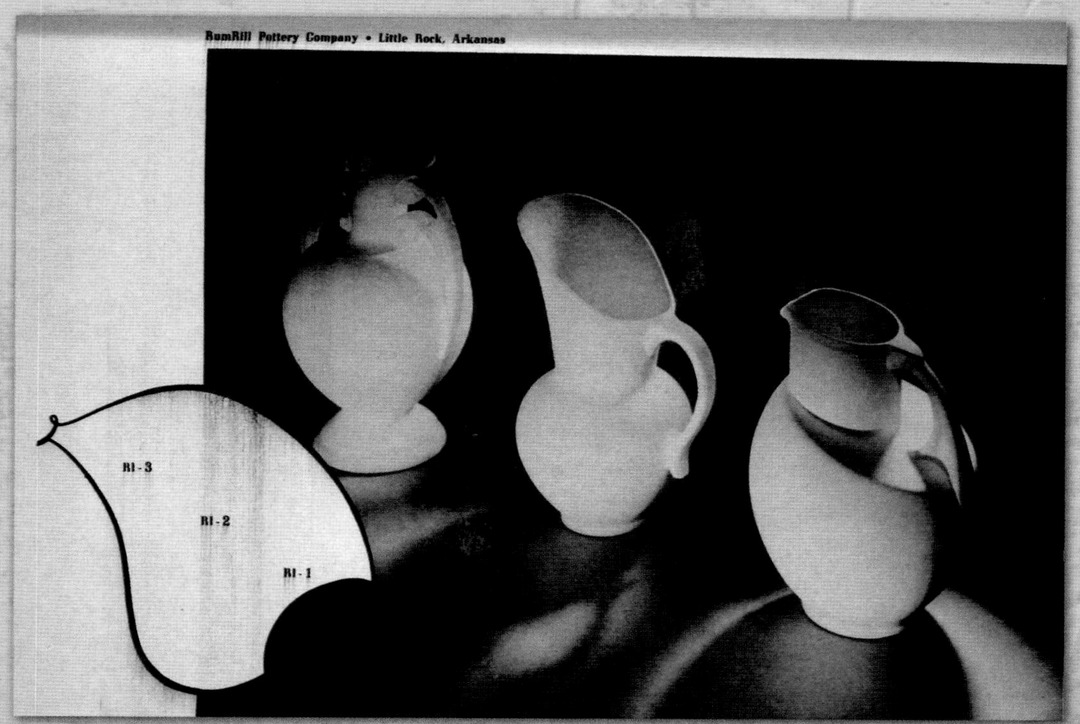
RumRill Pottery Company • Little Rock, Arkansas
RI-3
RI-2
RI-1

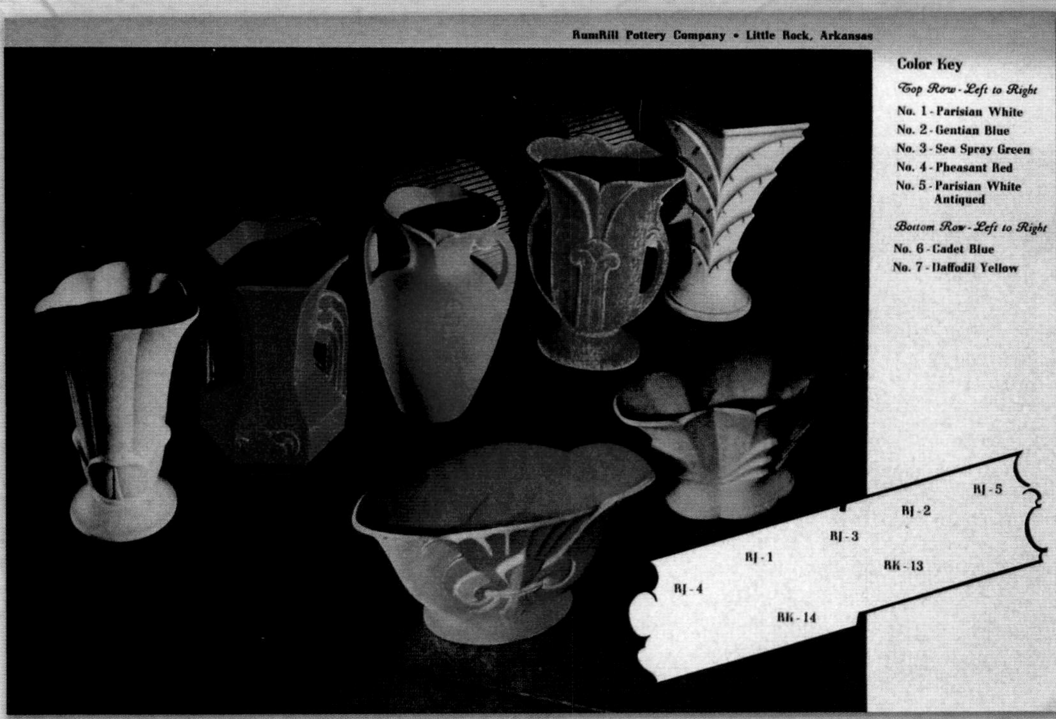
RumRill Pottery Company • Little Rock, Arkansas
Color Key
Top Row - Left to Right
No. 1 - Parisian White
No. 2 - Gentian Blue
No. 3 - Sea Spray Green
No. 4 - Pheasant Red
No. 5 - Parisian White Antiqued
Bottom Row - Left to Right
No. 6 - Cadet Blue
No. 7 - Daffodil Yellow
RJ - 5
RJ - 2
RJ - 3
RJ - 1
RK - 13
RJ - 4
RK - 14

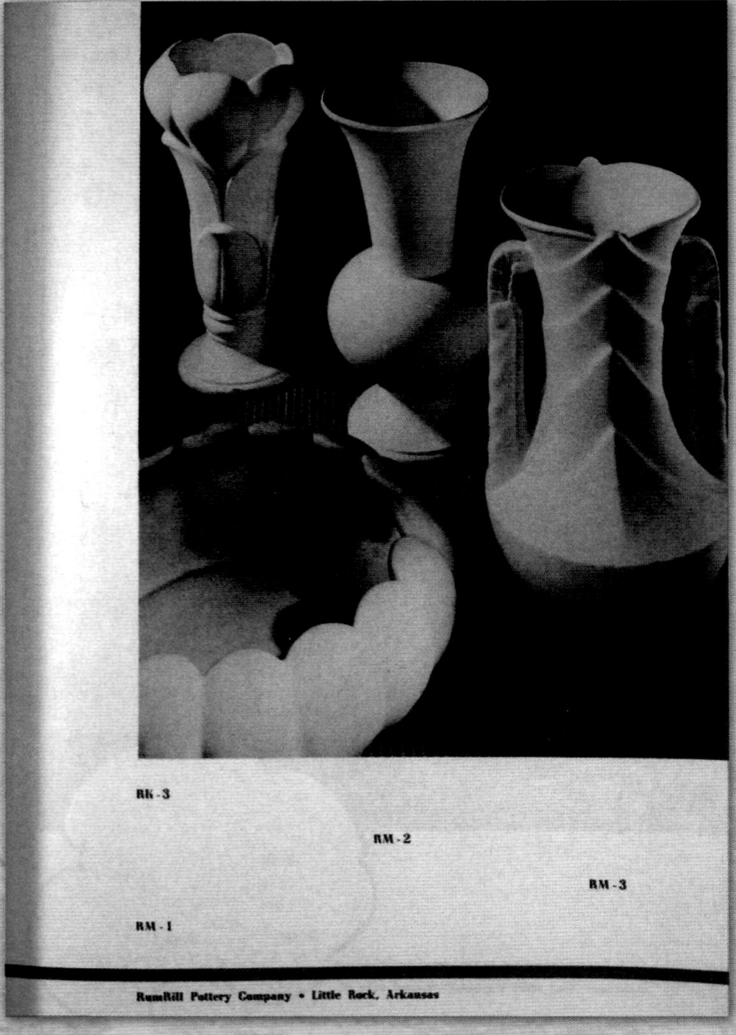
RK - 3
RM - 2
RM - 3
RM - 1
RumRill Pottery Company • Little Rock, Arkansas

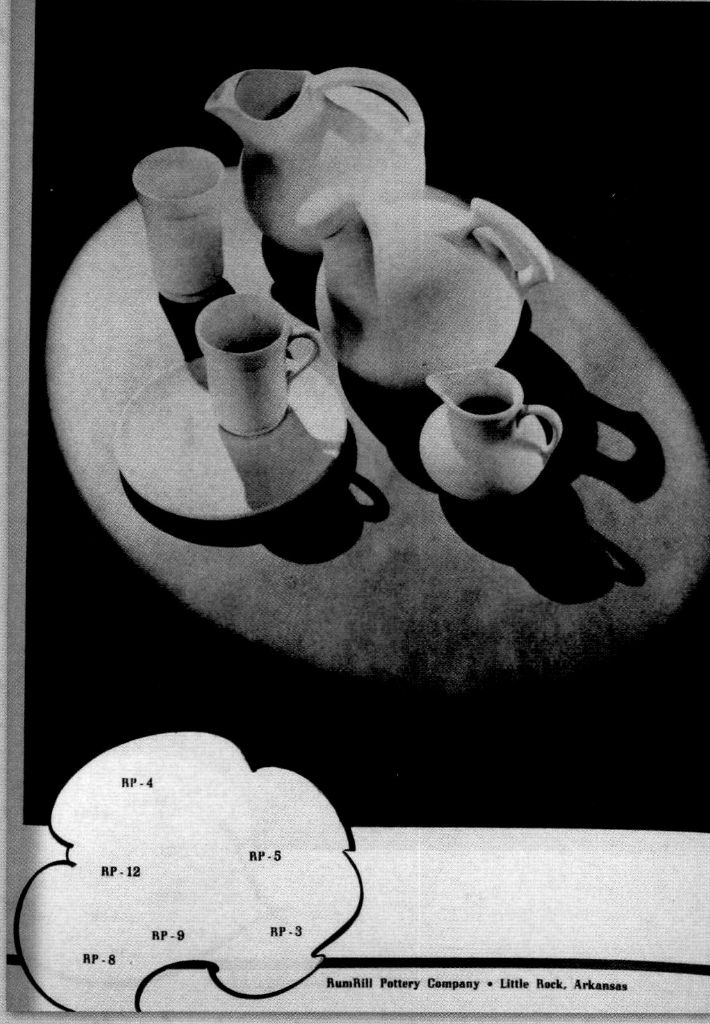

1938 RumRill catalog.

1938 RumRill catalog.

RumRill Pottery Company • Little Rock, Arkansas
RH-14
RK-14
RH-14

RumRill Pottery Company • Little Rock, Arkansas
RH-13
RK-13
RH-13

RumRill Art Pottery

PRICE LIST

RA—GROUP
No. 1—4¼" Vase
No. 2—4¼" "
No. 3—4¼" "
No. 5—4¼" "
No. 6—4¼" "
List Price—$2.50 per doz.

RB—GROUP
No. 1—3½" Ash Tray
No. 2—4¾" Vase
No. 3—4¾" "
No. 4—5 " "
No. 5—4¾" "
No. 6—4¾" "
List Price—$3.00 per doz.

RC—GROUP
No. 1—4 " Vase
No. 2—4½" "
No. 3—4½" "
No. 4—4½" "
No. 5—4¼" "
No. 7—4¼" "
No. 8—4¾" "
No. 9—4¾" "
No. 10—4¾" "
List Price—$4.80 per doz.

RD—GROUP
No. 1—5¼" Vase
No. 2—5¼" "
List Price—$4.80 per doz.

RE—GROUP
No. 1—6½" Vase
No. 2—6½" "
No. 3—6½" Vase
No. 4—6¼" "
No. 6—7¾" Oval Bowl
No. 8—7 " Bud Vase
No. 9—5 " Flower Pot
No. 10—6½" Bulb Bowl
No. 11—6¼" Vase
List Price—$6.00 per doz.

RF—GROUP
No. 1—8½" Vase
No. 2—7½" "
No. 3—7½" "
No. 4—8 " "
No. 5—7 " "
No. 6—6½" "
No. 7—7½" Bowl
No. 8—6 " Vase
No. 13—4¼" Candlestick
List Price—$9.60 per doz.

RG—GROUP
No. 1—6¾" Vase
No. 4—7½" "
No. 5—8 " "
List Price—$13.20 per doz.

RH—GROUP
No. 1—8¾" Vase
No. 2—8¾" "
No. 3—7½" "
No. 4—8¾" "
No. 5—9 " "
No. 6—8½" "
No. 7—8¾" "
No. 8—8¾" "
No. 9—8¾" "
No. 10—9½" "
No. 11—9 " Vase
No. 12—8¾" "
No. 13—8¾" "
No. 14—7½" "
No. 15—8¾" "
No. 16—9 " "
No. 17—8¾" "
No. 18—9 " "
List Price—$13.20 per doz.

RI—GROUP
No. 1— 8¾" Vase
No. 2— 9¾" "
No. 3—10¼" "
List Price—$18.00 per doz.

RJ—GROUP
No. 1—10¾" Vase
No. 2—11 " "
No. 3—11 " "
No. 4—10¾" "
No. 5—11 " "
No. 6—10½" Bowl
List Price—$24.00 per doz.

RK—GROUP
No. 3—12¾" Vase
No. 13—12½" Oval Bowl
No. 14—12½" " "
List Price—$24.00 per doz.

RL—GROUP
List Price—$36.00 per doz.

RM—GROUP
No. 1—13" Bowl
No. 2—13" Vase
No. 3—13" "
List Price—$42.00 per doz.

RO—GROUP
List Price—$48.00 per doz.

RS—GROUP
List Price—$60.00 per doz.

WRITE FOR DISCOUNTS

FLATWARE ACCESSORIES AND JUGS

PRICE LIST

	RP Group	All Colors Except Tangerine Per Dozen	Tangerine Per Dozen
Low Marmite—4½"	RP1	$3.36	$4.32
Sugar, open	RP2	3.36	4.32
Sugar, with cover	RP2	4.80	6.48
8 oz. Cream Pitcher	RP3	3.36	4.32
3 pt. Open Mouth Water Jug	RP4	12.00	13.20
2½ pt. Ball Jug with Cork	RP5	18.00	18.00
8 cup Coffee Server w/ Handle—no Top	RP6	14.40	14.40
8 cup Coffee Server with Top	RP6	16.80	16.80
3 pt. Batter Jug w/ Wood Handle	RP7	19.20	19.20
Char Plate—7"	RP8	2.40	3.36
7 oz. Pottery Handle Mug	RP9	3.36	4.32
10 oz. Pottery Handle Mug	RP10	4.08	5.04
7 oz. Plain Mug	RP11	2.40	3.36
10 oz. Plain Mug	RP12	3.12	4.08
7 oz. Wood Handle Mug	RP13	6.48	7.44
10 oz. Wood Handle Mug	RP14	7.20	8.16
Salt	RP15	3.12	4.08
Pepper	RP16	3.12	4.08
Syrup Pitcher w/ Cover	RP17	4.80	6.48
Plain Plate—7"	RP18	3.60	4.80

RumRill Art Pottery

RumRill Pottery Company

Little Rock, Arkansas

READ CAREFULLY

All shipments F. O. B. Zanesville, Ohio.

No allowance for transportation, drayage or storage.

A packing charge will be added to orders for less than $20.00.

BREAKAGE

Absolutely no allowance for breakage in transit. We employ only professional packers, and, in harmony with the policy of all crockery houses in the United States, we do not assume responsibility for breakage which occurs in transit. The Railroad Company assumes this responsibility and you can collect from them by pursuing the following course:

Call inspector or freight agent to inspect shipment immediately after unpacking.

Have him make notation of breakage on freight bill.

Send following papers to Railroad Company to support your claim:

Paid freight bill (with notation of breakage signed by freight agent).

Original Bill of Lading.

Original Invoice.

By following the above course you will have no difficulty in making collection.

SHORTAGE

All claims for shortage must be made within 5 days after receipt of merchandise.

Be sure to search packing thoroughly before writing us. Small pieces may easily be thrown out with packing materials.

RETURNED GOODS

We will ABSOLUTELY refuse to accept any goods returned to us unless the customer first secures our permission and agrees to pay the cost of packing, transportation and a 5% handling charge.

ROUTING

Designate whether shipment is to be made by parcel post, express or freight. Otherwise the Company will use its best judgment and will not be responsible for any additional expense incurred. Not responsible for goods delayed in transit.

C. O. D. shipments will not be made unless draft for at least one-third the amount of invoice accompanies the order.

IMPORTANT

To avoid mistakes order by shape number and finish number.

Early ordering is suggested as the wide range of shapes and colors makes it impracticable to carry complete stock at all times. The most careful attention is accorded all orders whether placed direct with the factory or through our representatives.

FREIGHT RATES
FROM OUR FACTORY AT ZANESVILLE, OHIO

RAILROAD

The following list of L. C. L. railroad freight rates has been compiled for the use of our customers. We cannot guarantee the correctness of these rates because they are changed at intervals by the carriers.

State	City	Per hundred lbs.
ALABAMA	Birmingham	$1.40
	Mobile	1.68
ARIZONA	Phoenix	3.14
ARKANSAS	Fort Smith	1.72
	Little Rock	1.56
CALIFORNIA	Los Angeles	3.14
	San Francisco	3.14
COLORADO	Denver	2.22
CONNECTICUT	Hartford	.99
DELAWARE	Wilmington	.85
DISTRICT OF COLUMBIA	Washington, D. C.	.78
FLORIDA	Jacksonville	1.72
	Miami	2.22
	St. Petersburg	1.97
	Tampa	2.01
GEORGIA	Atlanta	1.39
	Savannah	1.56
IDAHO	Boise	3.14
ILLINOIS	Chicago	.73
	Springfield	.80
	Peoria	.80
INDIANA	Evansville	.76
	Ft. Wayne	.58
	Indianapolis	.61
	Terre Haute	.68
IOWA	Cedar Rapids	1.02
	Des Moines	1.19
	Dubuque	.89
	Sioux City	1.40
	Waterloo	1.10
KANSAS	Kansas City	1.29
	Topeka	1.41
	Wichita	1.64
KENTUCKY	Louisville	.67
	Lexington	.62
LOUISIANA	New Orleans	1.80
MAINE	Portland	1.09
MARYLAND	Baltimore	.78
MASSACHUSETTS	Boston	1.05
	Worcester	1.05
MICHIGAN	Detroit	.58
	Grand Rapids	.70
	Saginaw	.68
MINNESOTA	Minneapolis	1.30
MISSISSIPPI	Jackson	1.61
MISSOURI	Kansas City	1.29
	St. Louis	.84
MONTANA	Butte	3.14
NEBRASKA	Lincoln	1.46
	Omaha	1.36
NEVADA	Reno	3.14
NEW HAMPSHIRE	Manchester	1.05
NEW JERSEY	Camden	.82
	Newark	.91
NEW MEXICO	Santa Fe	2.67
NEW YORK	Albany	.91
	Buffalo	.68
	New York	.91
	Rochester	.73
	Syracuse	.77
NORTH CAROLINA	Asheville	1.17
	Raleigh	1.03
NORTH DAKOTA	Bismark	2.01
OHIO	Cincinnati	.53
	Cleveland	.50
	Dayton	.47
OKLAHOMA	Oklahoma City	1.68
	Tulsa	1.55
OREGON	Portland	3.14
PENNSYLVANIA	Harrisburg	.76
	Philadelphia	.85
	Pittsburgh	.51
RHODE ISLAND	Providence	1.05
SOUTH CAROLINA	Columbia	1.42
SOUTH DAKOTA	Sioux Falls	1.44
TENNESSEE	Memphis	1.31
	Nashville	1.11
TEXAS	Dallas	1.85
	Ft. Worth	1.85
	San Antonio	2.16
UTAH	Salt Lake City	3.10
VERMONT	Burlington	1.05
VIRGINIA	Norfolk	.92
	Richmond	.86
WASHINGTON	Seattle	3.14
	Spokane	3.14
WEST VIRGINIA	Charleston	.52
	Clarksburg	.53
	Wheeling	.44
WISCONSIN	Green Bay	.95
	Milwaukee	.80
	Racine	.78
WYOMING	Cheyenne	2.19

The following Rates for L. C. L. shipments to the destinations named are made by the WESTERN FREIGHT ASSOCIATION, 1390 East Seventh Street, Los Angeles, California.

Destination	Rate per 100 lbs.
Boise, Idaho Butte, Montana El Paso, Texas Los Angeles, California Phoenix, Arizona Portland, Oregon Salt Lake City, Utah San Francisco, California Seattle, Washington Spokane, Washington	$1.95

Destination	Rates per 100 lbs.
Dallas, Texas	$1.77
Denver, Colorado	1.65
Fort Worth, Texas	1.77
San Antonio, Texas	1.60

The Western Freight Association maintains an office in each of the above cities and serves all points in Arizona, California, Colorado, Idaho, Montana, Nevada, New Mexico, Oregon, Washington, Utah and Texas. Customers in these states should communicate with their closest office for rate information.

Carload rates will be furnished on request.

1938 RumRill catalog.

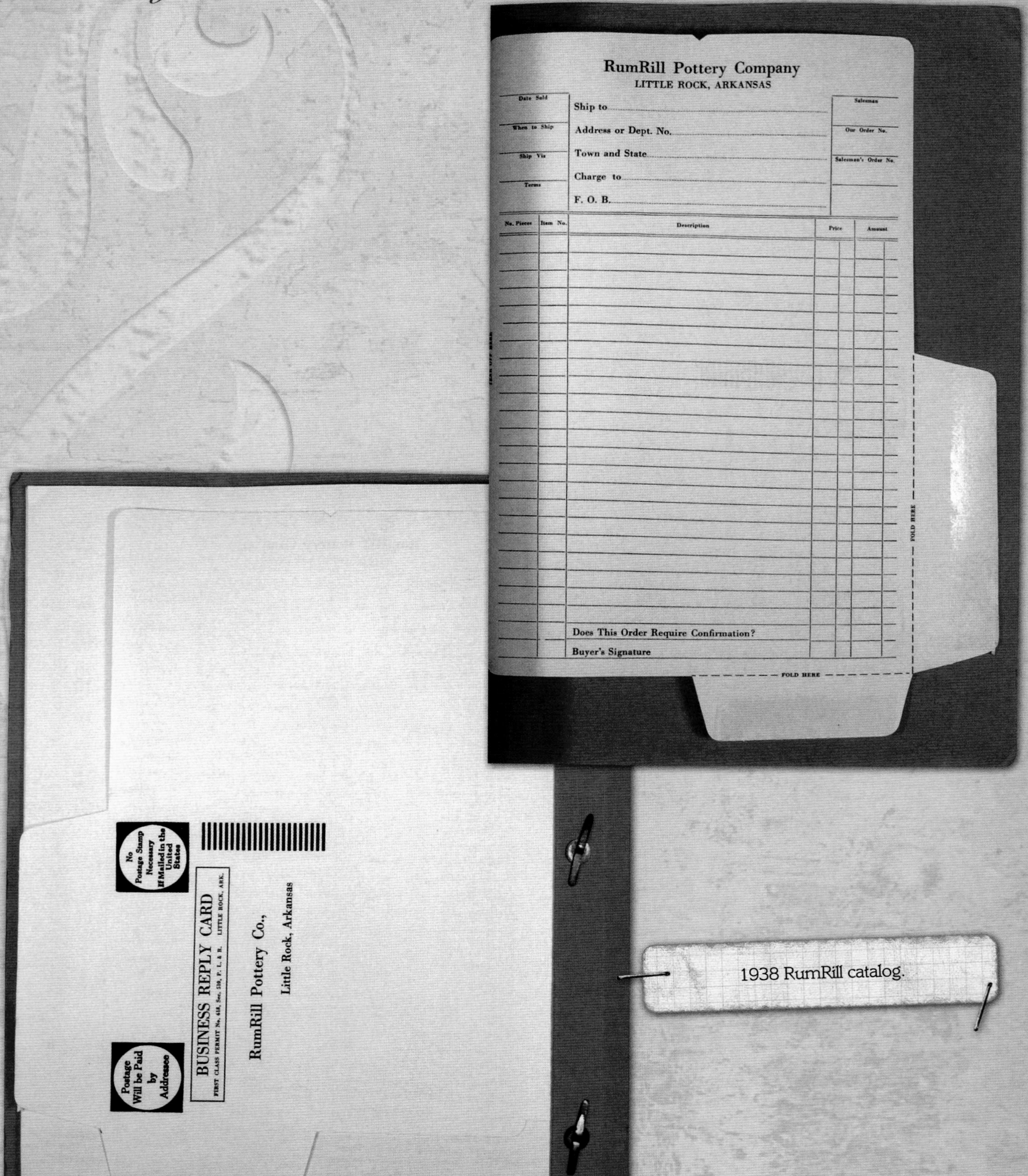

RumRill Pottery Company
LITTLE ROCK, ARKANSAS

Date Sold
When to Ship
Ship Via
Terms

Ship to
Address or Dept. No.
Town and State
Charge to
F. O. B.

Salesman
Our Order No.
Salesman's Order No.

No. Pieces	Item No.	Description	Price	Amount
		Does This Order Require Confirmation?		
		Buyer's Signature		

FOLD HERE

FOLD HERE

No Postage Stamp Necessary If Mailed in the United States

BUSINESS REPLY CARD
FIRST CLASS PERMIT No. 418, Sec. 510, P. L. & R. LITTLE ROCK, ARK.

Postage Will be Paid by Addressee

RumRill Pottery Co.,
Little Rock, Arkansas

1938 RumRill catalog.

RUMRILL PRICES

GROUP	
RA	.84
RB	1.05
RC	1.32
RD	1.50
RE	1.80
RF	2.40
RG	3.00
RH	3.60
RI	4.80
RJ	6.00
RK	7.20
RL	9.00
RM	12.00
RS	15.00
RT	18.00

	Others	Tange
RP 1 Marmite	1.68 Doz.	2.16 dz.
RP 2 Suger, no cover	1.68	2.16
RP 2 Sugar, With cover	2.40	3.24
RP 3 Creamer	1.68	2.16
RP 6 Coffee Server With wood handle	7.20 without cover	
	8.40 with cover	
RP 7 Batter Jug with handle	9.60	
RP 8 Chocolate Plate	1.20	1.68
RP 9 7 oz. mug pot handle	1.68	2.16
RP 10 10 oz Mug pot handle	2.04	2.52
RP 11 Mug no handle 7 oz	1.20	1.68
RP 12 " 10 oz	1.56	2.14
RP 13 Mug wood handle 7 oz	3.24	3.72
RP 14 " " " 10 oz	3.60	4.08
RP 15 Salt Shaker	1.56	2.04
RP 16 Pepper Shaker	1.56	2.04
RP 17 Syrup Pitcher	2.40	3.24
Tray	.40	

~~xxxxRRxxxxxxxxx~~

RP 4 Open mouth Water jug	4.50 doz	5.04 doz
RP 5 Cork Water Jug	all colors 48¢ ea	

RP 4 & RP 5 are net prices

Package charge on orders less than $12.00 - 6% - minimum chg. 25¢

DELUXE ASSORTMENT

12 Pcs. RA - Group - Size $4\frac{1}{4}$"
(2 Ea. RA1, RA2, RA5 - 3 Ea. RA3, RA 6)

12 Pcs. RB - Group - Size 4 3/4"
(2 EA. RB1, RB2, RB3, RB4, RB5, RB6)

12 Pcs. RC-D - Group - Size $4\frac{1}{2}$" - 4 3/4"
(1 Ea. RC1, 2, 3, 4, 5, 7, 8, 9, 10 - 1RD2, 2RD1)

12 Pcs RE - Group - Size $6\frac{1}{2}$"
(2 Ea. RE2, RE3, RE1, RE5, RE4, RE19)

12 Pcs. RH - Group - Size $7\frac{1}{2}$" - 9"
(2 Ea. RH14, RH23, RH24, RH25, RH26, RH27)

6 Pcs. RI - Group - Size $7\frac{1}{2}$" - 8 3/4"
(2 RI4, 2 RI5, 2 RI6)

4 RJ11 - Candlesticks

2 RJ9 - Vase - Size 10"

2 RJ10, Vase - Size 10"

2 RK1 - Vase - Size 12"

2 RK2 - Vase - Size 12"

2 RL1 - Vase - Size 12"

2 RL2 - Vase - Size 11"

2 RL3 - Vase - Size 11"

2 RL4 - Vase - Size 12"

2 RL5 - Vase - Size 12"

2 RM6 - Bowl - Size $8\frac{1}{2}$"

2 RM7 - Vase - Size 12 3/4"

These lists show the RumRill prices for Shawnee-made pieces.

RumRill
Pottery Company
"Every Piece Built For A Purpose"

LITTLE ROCK
ARKANSAS

White Drum
Orange, Massachussetts

March 5, 1940

Gentlemen:

Your friendship and your business is very important to us.

I have persuaded our company that we should make it easier for you to mail order. This circular is the result.

I will certainly regard it as a personal favor if you will give us your reaction as to the value of this idea; add any comments you wish to make and send to us in the enclosed envelope. Thank you and may we hear from you in the very near future.

Best regards and good luck.

Jack Rumrill
Assistant Sales Manager

ae

Mantel Ensemble

This graceful mantel ensemble is particularly adaptable to mantels with large Venetian mirrors above them.

Buffet Ensemble

This full-curved and gay looking ensemble adds an atmosphere of gaiety and hospitality to a dining room.

Table Ensemble

This dignified and formal ensemble makes an ideal set for hall tables and other formal arrangements.

LET THE **POWER OF SUGGESTION** MAKE **MORE MONEY** FOR YOU

Make more money from pottery! You can do this by arranging neat tables or shelves according to groups in the same price range and by placing a neat price card on each group. . . . Many a time your customer looks at the attractive vases—yet hesitates to buy because of fear that the price may be more than anticipated. But, with the pottery neatly displayed and clearly priced, this same customer will immediately see which group or item fits his or her pocketbook and will step up and buy without having to ask any questions. . . . Let the power of suggestion work for you! Streamline your merchandising of pottery and you will be amazed at the increased merchandise turnover. . . . Take advantage of this profitable market today by preparing an eye-appeal and purse-appeal pottery display! . . . And remember—RumRill pottery is a most appropriate gift for any occasion. So why not display it throughout the year and make more profit!

A fold-out advertising flyer dated March 1940, which surprisingly lists George Rumrill's son, Jack, as the company's assistant sales manager.

Mantel (Above)
H14—Horn
K14—Bowl
Buffet
E14—Sticks
J6—Bowl
Table
I-15—Bowl
I-17—Candle St
A-7
A-1
A-2
A-3
A-6
A-5
B-8
B-1
B-6
B-4
B-3
B-5
E-19
E-12
E-18
E-17
E-3
E-1
E-5
E-4
F-2
F-5
F-1
F-16

1940 RumRill flyer.

From the desk of Lawton Gonder — Gonder Copy

New Shapes 1940

A7 - Hi Hat.
B9 - Miniature Candle
D10 - " Basket
E7 - " Log.
E17 - " Well
E38 - Fruit Bowl.
E50 - Rock
F14 - Basket
16 - Vase - (figure) old 26
17 - " " old 27
H31 - Fruit Bowl
32 - Vase (as E5)
33 - " (as M4)
34 - Pitcher Vase
35 - Vase (I-6)
36 - Hat Bowl.
37 - Pottery Shop.
38 - Vase (Four Petals)
39 - Basket (leaf)
41 - Fluted Bowl
42 - " Vase

This note from Lawton Gonder's desk shows the proposed new shapes for 1940. The handwriting at the top is Lawton Gonder's.

New York Display
Room 410
225 Fifth Avenue

These new and intriguing designs are an addition to our regular catalog.

We have created a new and different art Pottery which makes an unusual contribution to the artistry that can be utilized by the skilled hands of master Pottery craftsmen. It is by this policy of constant development of new shapes and colors that we have made RumRill Art Pottery Co. the outstanding profitable merchandise for our customers.

Our Pottery comes in the following Finishes and Colors:

No. 1—White
No. 2—Gentian Blue
No. 3—Sea Spray Green
No. 4—Forest Fire
No. 5—Mandarin Blue
No. 6—Cadet Blue
No. 7—Daffodil Yellow
No. 8—Forest Green
No. 9—Ashes of Roses

There is a difference in White. We call your attention to the unique soft and velvety surface and deep rich texture never before attained in Ceramic Arts.

PRICE LIST

A	Group List Price	$ 3.00 Per Doz.
B	" " "	3.60 " "
C	" " "	4.80 " "
D	" " "	4.80 " "
E	" " "	6.00 " "
F	" " "	9.60 " "
G	" " "	13.20 " "
H	" " "	13.20 " "
I	Group List Price	$18.00 Per Doz.
J	" " "	24.00 " "
K	" " "	30.00 " "
L	" " "	36.00 " "
M	" " "	42.00 " "
O	" " "	48.00 " "
S	" " "	60.00 " "

Usual Discounts Apply

RUMRILL POTTERY COMPANY, LITTLE ROCK, ARKANSAS

The Modern Line and Rustic Group (Rock Garden) series were handsomely marketed in this catalog that was also introduced in 1940.

—O-3 - GARDEN GATE
I-10 - LOG CANDLESTICKS, Pr.
K-16 - STUMP IVY JAR
I-9 - LOG CENTER BOWL

Bottom—F-10 - STONE BOX
I-11 - TWO TIER ROCK GARDEN
I-12 - ROCK CANDLESTICKS, Pr.

I-8 - WELL WALL POCKET
I-7 - WELL IVY BOWL
S-4 - THREE TIER ROCK GARDEN

RumRill Pottery Company • Little Rock, Arkansas

1940 supplemental catalog.

S-3 - MODERN CAT
K-15 - QUAD CYLINDRICAL VASE
L-6 - MODERN BOWL
J-23 - MODERN CANDLESTICKS
L-7 - MODERN HEAD VASE

RumRill Pottery Company • Little Rock, Arkansas

ILLUSTRATED on the following pages are the new RumRill lines of art and specialty pottery for 1941. Also listed are the attractive prices, and a new conception of merchandising in the pottery industry. • Ever since our first year in business, our production volume has constantly increased. We believe this steady growth has been built by strict adherence to a sales policy based on sound business. This policy insists upon . . . established price values . . . artistically and practically shaped articles . . . colors and finishes in tune with the mode-creative-advanced and popular . . . products of highest quality which can be produced only by the better materials shaped by the skilled hands of master pottery craftsmen . . . prompt service and attention to details . . . and sales plans that assist our customers in building bigger profits through increased volume and faster turnover. • Recently discovered materials demand a secret process of manufacture and represent the latest achievements in ceramic engineering. They produce a pure white body, which when fired to exact temperatures, are more durable than ordinary earthenwares. Our glazes in both matt and bright glazes, are beautiful tones of popular colors. They are so compounded and fired that crazing and checking are practically eliminated. Both ink and pencil marks can be easily removed from our matt glazes with a damp cloth, and each piece will pass this rigid test. • As a result of these outstanding improvements, it has been necessary to install additional equipment to meet our requirements. To complete this plan of individualized sales-service we now offer "private brand" merchandise. On orders totalling more than $150 we will affix your own labels at no increase in price. • Study this plan carefully and compare it with any other from the standpoint of quality, design, and profit to you. Then place your order today.

RumRill
Pottery Company

LITTLE ROCK ARKANSAS

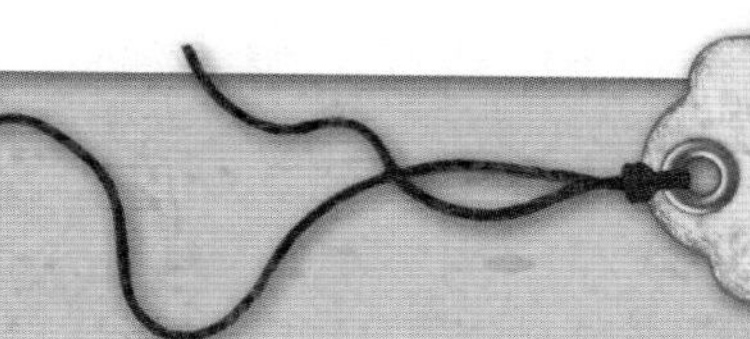

Front cover and inside page of the first 1941 catalog. The Silver Gray finish is shown in this catalog.

RumRill Art Pottery

RumRill Pottery Company

Little Rock, Arkansas

READ CAREFULLY

All shipments F.O.B. Mt. Gilead, Ohio.

No allowance for transportation, drayage or storage.

A packing charge will be added to orders for less than $25.00.

BREAKAGE

Absolutely no allowance for breakage in transit. We employ only professional packers, and, in harmony with the policy of all crockery houses in the United States, we do not assume responsibility for breakage which occurs in transit. The railroad company assumes this responsibility and you can collect from them by pursuing the following course:

Call inspector or freight agent to inspect shipment immediately after unpacking.

Have him make notation of breakage on freight bill.

Send following papers to Railroad Company to support your claim:

Paid freight bill (with notation of breakage signed by freight agent).

Original Bill of Lading.

Original Invoice.

By following the above course you will have no difficulty in making collection.

SHORTAGE

All claims for shortage must be made within 5 days after receipt of merchandise.

Be sure to search packing thoroughly before writing us. Small pieces may easily be thrown out with packing materials.

RETURNED GOODS

We will ABSOLUTELY refuse to accept any goods returned to us unless the customer first secures our permission and agrees to pay the cost of packing, transportation and a 5% handling charge.

ROUTING

Designate whether shipment is to be made by parcel post, express or freight. Otherwise the Company will use its best judgment and will not be responsible for any additional expense incurred. Not responsible for goods delayed in transit.

C.O.D. shipments will not be made unless draft for at least one-third the amount of invoice accompanies the order.

IMPORTANT

To avoid mistakes order by shape number and finish number.

Early ordering is suggested as the wide range of shapes and colors makes it impracticable to carry complete stock at all times. The most careful attention is accorded all orders whether placed direct with the factory or through our representatives.

PRICE LIST (Subject to Change Without Notice)

"A" Items—4½-in. .... $1.50 Doz. Net
A1; A2; A3; A5; A6; A7; A8; A9; A10; A112.

"B" Items—4¾-in. .... $1.80 Doz. Net
B1; B2; B3; B4; B5; B6; B7; B8; B10; B11; B12; B13; B14; B15; B16; B17; B18; B20.

"C" Items—5-in. .... $2.40 Doz. Net
C1; C2; C3; C4; C5; C7; C8; C9; C10; C11 pr.; C19.

"D" Items—5-in. .... $2.40 Doz. Net
D1; D2; D10; D20; D21.

"E" Items—6½-in. .... $3.00 Doz. Net
E1; E2; E3; E4; E5; E7; E8; E10; E11; E12; E13 ea.; E14 ea.; E15; E16; E17; E18; E19; E20; E21; E38; E39; E40; E41; E42; E43; E44; E45; E46; E48; E50; E103ea.

"F" Items—7½-in. .... $4.80 Doz. Net
F1; F2; F3; F4; F5; F6; F7; F8; F9; F10; F13 Ea.; F14; F16; F17; F18; F19; F20; F21; F22; F23; F24; F110.

"G" Items—7½-in. .... $4.80 Doz. Net
G1; G2; G4; G5; G6; G7; G8; G9.

"H" Items—9-in. .... $6.00 Doz. Net
H1; H2; H3; H4; H5; H6; H7; H8; H9; H10; H11; H12; H13; H14; H15; H16; H17; H18; H19; H20; H21; H23; H29; H30; H31; H32; H33; H34; H35; H36; H37; H38; H39; H40; H41; H42; H43; H44; H45; H46; H47; H48; H49; H51; H52; H53; H54; H55; H56; H57; H58; H59 pr.

"I" Items—10¾-in. .... $9.00 Doz. Net
I-1; I-2; I-3; I-5; I-6; I-7; I-8; I-9; I-10 pr.; I-11; I-12 pr.; I-13; I-14; I-15; I-16 pr.; I-17 pr.; I-18; I-19; I-20; I-23; I-24; I-25; I-26; I-27; I-40; I-45.

"J" Items—11-in. .... $12.00 Doz. Net
J1; J2; J3; J4; J5; J6; J7; J8; J9; J10; J11; J12; J13; J14; J15; J16; J17; J18; J19; J20; J22 pr.; J23 pr.; J24; J25; J26; J27; J29; J30; J31; J32; J33; J34; J35; J36; J37; J38; J39; J50.

"K" Items—12½-in. .... $15.00 Doz. Net
K1; K2; K3; K5; K6; K7; K8; K13; K14.

"L" Items—13-in. .... $18.00 Doz. Net
L1; L2; L3; L4; L5; L7; L8; L9; L10; L11; L12.

"M" Items—14-in. .... $21.00 Doz. Net
M1; M2; M3; M4; M5; M7; M8; M10; M19; M40.

"S" Items—15-in. .... $30.00 Doz. Net
S3; S4; S5; S6; S7; S8.

"T" Items—16-in. .... $36.00 Doz. Net
T1; T2.

"X" Items—18½-in. .... $45.00 Doz. Net
X1; X2.

"R-100" Planter Items
R101; R103; R105.

"R-200" Planter Items
R201; R202; R203; R204; R206; R207; R208; R210; R211.

"R-300" Planter Items
R303; R307; R309; R310; R311.

"P" Items	Doz.
P 1—Low Marmite 4½-in.	$2.16
P 2—Sugar, no cover	2.16
P 2—Sugar with cover	3.00
P 3—Creamer	2.10
P 4—Open Water Jug	6.60
P 6—Coffee Server	9.00
P 7—Batter Jug	10.50
P11—7-oz. Mug	1.50
P12—10-oz. Mug	2.04
P17—Syrup Pitcher	3.24
P19—Cup, Coffee	2.10
P20—Saucer, Coffee	1.50
P21—Range Jar	3.00
P22—Salt	2.10
P23—Pepper	2.10
P24—Cookie Jar	7.20
P25—5-in. Mixing Bowl	1.20
P26—6-in. Mixing Bowl	1.50
P27—7-in. Mixing Bowl	2.40
P28—8-in. Mixing Bowl	3.00
P29—9-in. Mixing Bowl	3.90

FINISHES

All items may be had in the following finishes:

1—Parisian White
3—Sea Spray Green
6—Cadet Blue
7—Daffodil Yellow
9—Burgundy Red
10—Cameo (Peach)
14—Silver Gray

Items J—K—L—M—S—T and X may also be had in:

15—White Antique
16—Green Antique

A 20% additional charge is necessary on: Items A, B, C, D, E, F, G and H—in No. 15 and No. 16 Finishes.

The second printing of this catalog had the addition of the new 1941 slogan, "The Staple Line of Pottery." This slogan appears right under the dealer sign. Note that the Silver Gray finish is omitted from the available finishes.

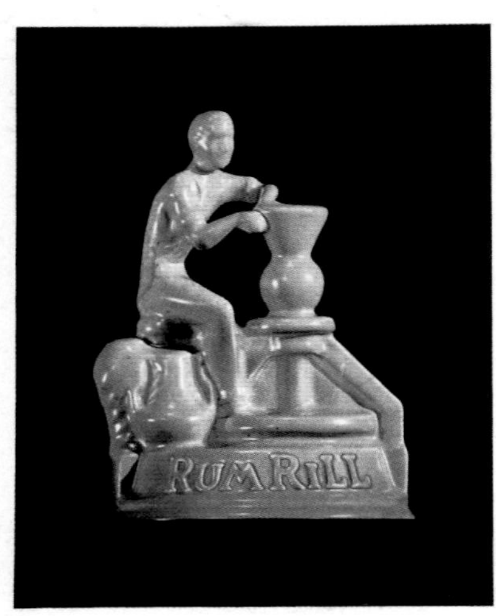

ILLUSTRATED on the following pages are the new RumRill lines of art and specialty pottery for 1941. Also listed are the attractive prices, and a new conception of merchandising in the pottery industry. ● Ever since our first year in business, our production volume has constantly increased. We believe this steady growth has been built by strict adherence to a sales policy based on sound business. This policy insists upon . . . established price values . . . artistically and practically shaped articles . . . colors and finishes in tune with the mode-creative-advanced and popular . . . products of highest quality which can be produced only by the better materials shaped by the skilled hands of master pottery craftsmen . . . prompt service and attention to details . . . and sales plans that assist our customers in building bigger profits through increased volume and faster turnover. ● Recently discovered materials demand a secret process of manufacture and represent the latest achievements in ceramic engineering. They produce a pure white body, which when fired to exact temperatures, are more durable than ordinary earthenwares. Our glazes in both matt and bright glazes, are beautiful tones of popular colors. They are so compounded and fired that crazing and checking are practically eliminated. Both ink and pencil marks can be easily removed from our matt glazes with a damp cloth, and each piece will pass this rigid test. ● As a result of these outstanding improvements, it has been necessary to install additional equipment to meet our requirements. To complete this plan of individualized sales-service we now offer "private brand" merchandise. On orders totalling more than $150 we will affix your own labels at no increase in price. ● Study this plan carefully and compare it with any other from the standpoint of quality, design, and profit to you. Then place your order today.

"The Staple Line of Pottery"

L I T T L E

C 1
C 2
C 3
C 4
C 5
C 8
C 7
C 9
C 10
D 21
D 20
C 19
D 2
E 41
E 40
C 11
E 43
E 21
E 38
E 17
D 1
D 10
E 42
E 39
E 50
E 44
E 1
E 2
E 3
E 4
E 5
E 11
E 20
E 18
E 46
E 48
E 45
E 103
E 13
E 14
E 15
E 10
E 19
E 7
F 9
F 10

1941 RumRill catalog.

H 1
H 2
H 3
H 4
H 5
H 6
H 7
H 8
H 9
H 10
H 11
H 12
H 13
H 14
H 15
H 16
H 17
H 18
H 23
H 33
H 19
H 35
H 29
H 30
H 31
H 32
H 20
H 34
H 21
H 36

H 48
H 37
H 49
H 39
H 57
H 38
H 44
H 41
H 45
H 42
H 46
H 43
H 58
H 40
H 47
H 51
H 52
H 53
H 54
H 55
H 56
I-1
I-2
I-3
I-5
I-6
I-7
I-14
I-8
I-18

1941 RumRill catalog.

1941 RumRill catalog.

K 2
K 5
K 8
K 3
K 14
K 6
K 7
K 13
L 12
L 9
L 10
L 1
L 2
L 5
L 4
L 3
L 7
L 11
L 8
M 1
M 40
M 19

M 2
M 3
M 4
M 5
M 7
M 8
M 10

P 1
P 2
P 3
P 12
P 11
P 17
P 21
P 4
P 7
P 22
P 23
P 6
P 24
P 29
P 28
P 27
P 26
P 25
P 19
P 20

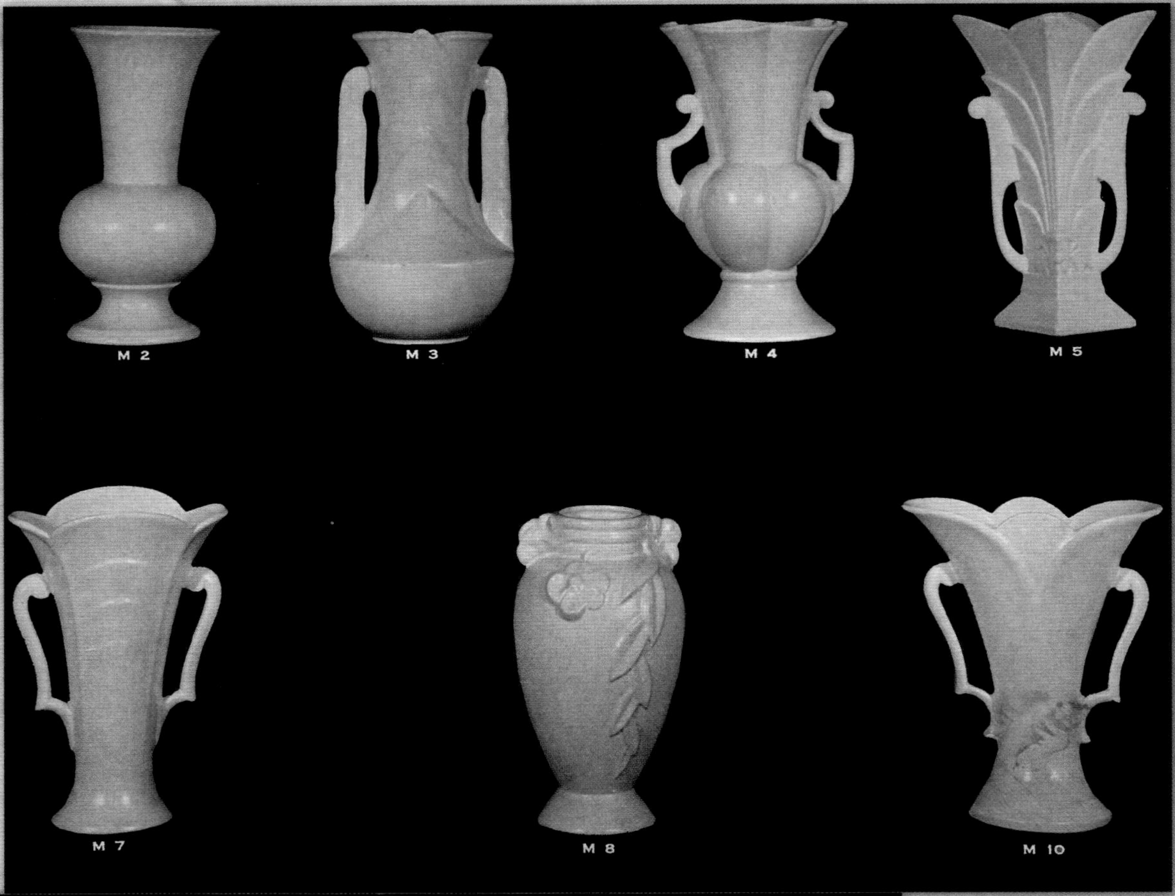

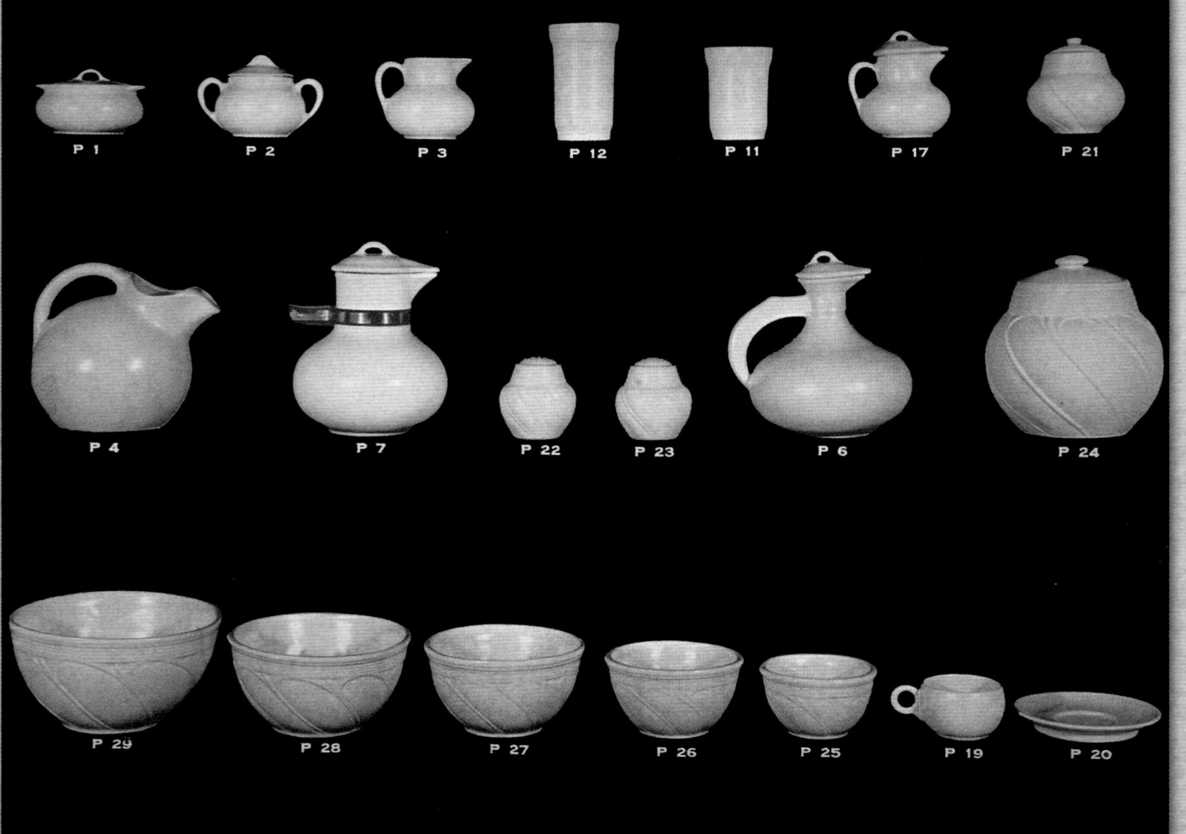

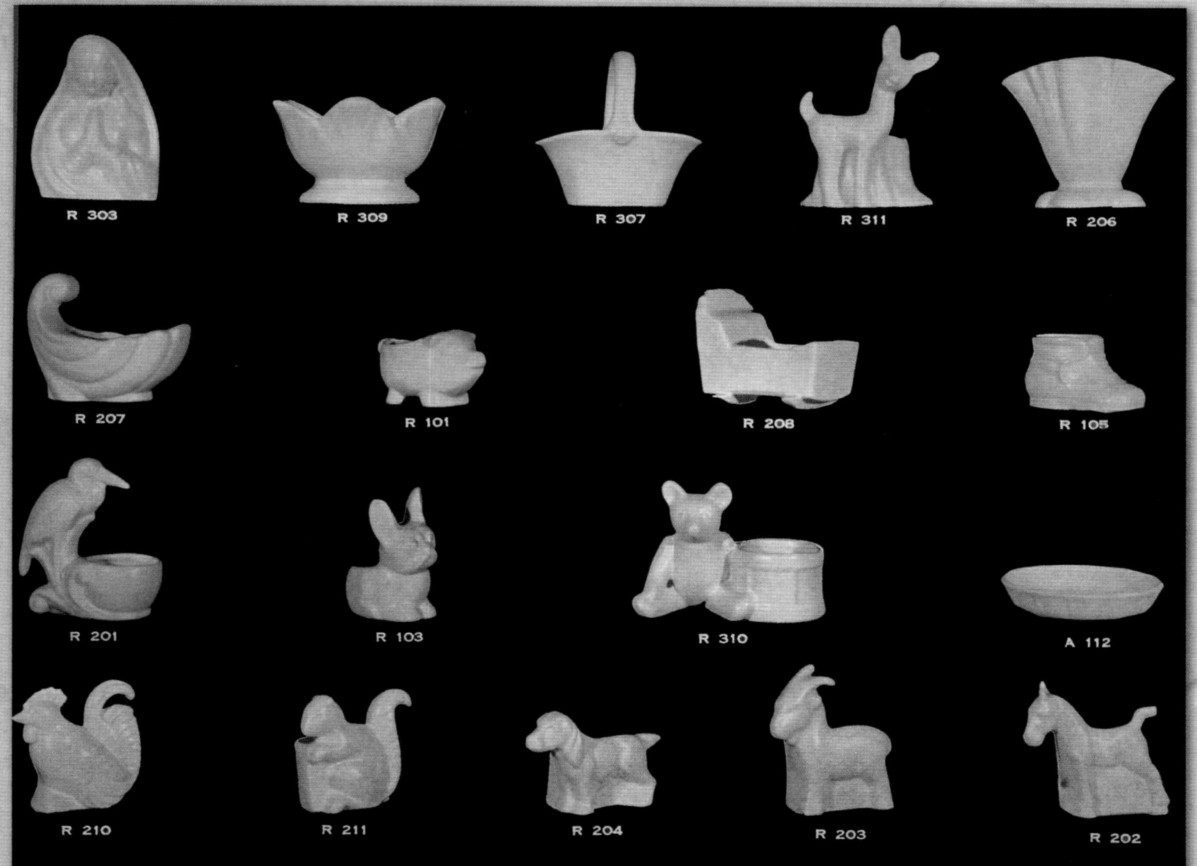

S 6 S 5 S 4

X 1 X 2

1941 RumRill catalog.

Upper ensemble:
Log E 7
Candlesticks C 11

Lower ensemble:
Swan B 14
Bowl A 112
Petal Bowl E 41
Plate E 42

Upper ensemble:
Candlesticks I-16
Bowl I-13

Lower ensemble:
Horns H 14
Bowl K 14

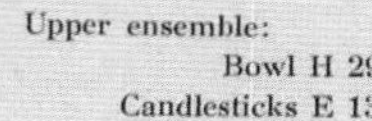

Upper ensemble:
Bowl H 29
Candlesticks E 13

Lower ensemble:
Bowl H 19
Candlesticks E 14

Bowl H 44
Bird in Bowl B 10
Bird Outside Bowl B 11

Bowl H 45
Candlesticks E 103

Upper ensemble:
Log I-9
Candlesticks I-10

Lower ensemble:
Bowl J 39
Candlesticks H 59

Bowl K 13
Candlesticks F 13

Upper ensemble:
Hurricane Jug H 30
Bowl J 6

Lower ensemble:
Italian Pitcher J 29
Bowl M 1

Upper ensemble:
Bowl H 41
Vases H 42

Lower ensemble:
Pitcher I-26
Bowl I-25

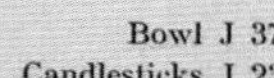

Bowl J 37
Candlesticks J 23

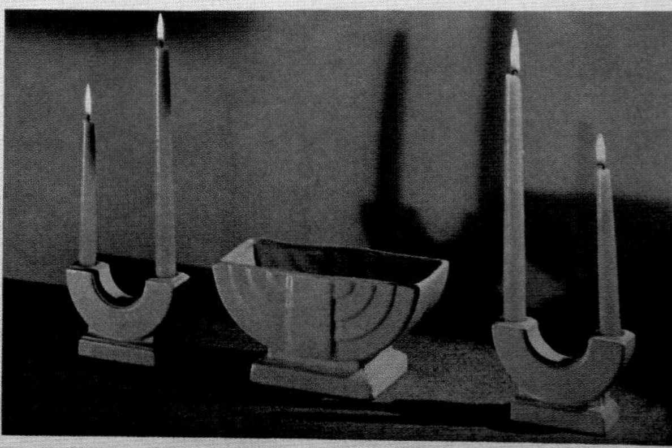

Bowl I-15 Candlesticks I-17

RumRill Art Pottery

RumRill Pottery Company

Little Rock, Arkansas

READ CAREFULLY

All shipments F.O.B. Mt. Gilead, Ohio.

No allowance for transportation, drayage or storage.

A packing charge will be added to orders for less than $25.00.

BREAKAGE

Absolutely no allowance for breakage in transit. We employ only professional packers, and, in harmony with the policy of all crockery houses in the United States, we do not assume responsibility for breakage which occurs in transit. The railroad company assumes this responsibility and you can collect from them by pursuing the following course:

Call inspector or freight agent to inspect shipment immediately after unpacking.

Have him make notation of breakage on freight bill.

Send following papers to Railroad Company to support your claim:

Paid freight bill (with notation of breakage signed by freight agent).

Original Bill of Lading.

Original Invoice.

By following the above course you will have no difficulty in making collection.

SHORTAGE

All claims for shortage must be made within 5 days after receipt of merchandise.

Be sure to search packing thoroughly before writing us. Small pieces may easily be thrown out with packing materials.

RETURNED GOODS

We will ABSOLUTELY refuse to accept any goods returned to us unless the customer first secures our permission and agrees to pay the cost of packing, transportation and a 5% handling charge.

ROUTING

Designate whether shipment is to be made by parcel post, express or freight. Otherwise the Company will use its best judgment and will not be responsible for any additional expense incurred. Not responsible for goods delayed in transit.

C.O.D. shipments will not be made unless draft for at least one-third the amount of invoice accompanies the order.

IMPORTANT

To avoid mistakes order by shape number and finish number.

Early ordering is suggested as the wide range of shapes and colors makes it impracticable to carry complete stock at all times. The most careful attention is accorded all orders whether placed direct with the factory or through our representatives.

PRICE LIST (Subject to Change Without Notice)

"A" Items—4½-in. ....$1.50 Doz. Net
A1; A2; A3; A5; A6; A7; A8; A9; A10; A112.

"B" Items—4¾-in. ....$1.80 Doz. Net
B1; B2; B3; B4; B5; B6; B7; B8; B10; B11; B12; B13; B14; B15; B16; B17; B18; B20.

"C" Items—5-in. ....$2.40 Doz. Net
C1; C2; C3; C4; C5; C7; C8; C9; C10; C11 pr.; C19.

"D" Items—5-in. ....$2.40 Doz. Net
D1; D2; D10; D20; D21.

"E" Items—6½-in. ....$3.00 Doz. Net
E1; E2; E3; E4; E5; E7; E8; E10; E11; E12; E13 ea.; E14 ea.; E15; E16; E17; E18; E19; E20; E21; E38; E39; E40; E41; E42; E43; E44; E45; E46; E48; E50; E103ea.

"F" Items—7½-in. ....$4.80 Doz. Net
F1; F2; F3; F4; F5; F6; F7; F8; F9; F10; F13 Ea.; F14; F16; F17; F18; F19; F20; F21; F22; F23; F24; F110 ea.

"G" Items—7½-in. ....$4.80 Doz. Net
G1; G2; G4; G5; G6; G7; G8; G9.

"H" Items—9-in. ....$6.00 Doz. Net
H1; H2; H3; H4; H5; H6; H7; H8; H9; H10; H11; H12; H13; H14; H15; H16; H17; H18; H19; H20; H21; H23; H29; H30; H31; H32; H33; H34; H35; H36; H37; H38; H39; H40; H41; H42; H43; H44; H45; H46; H47; H48; H49; H51; H52; H53; H54; H55; H56; H57; H58; H59 pr.

"I" Items—10¼-in. ....$9.00 Doz. Net
I-1; I-2; I-3; I-5; I-6; I-7; I-8; I-9; I-10 pr.; I-11; I-12 pr.; I-13; I-14; I-15; I-16 pr.; I-17 pr.; I-18; I-19; I-20; I-23; I-24; I-25; I-26; I-27; I-40; I-45.

"J" Items—11-in. ....$12.00 Doz. Net
J1; J2; J3; J4; J5; J6; J7; J8; J9; J10; J11; J12; J13; J14; J15; J16; J17; J18; J19; J20; J22 pr.; J23 pr.; J24; J25; J26; J27; J29; J30; J31; J32; J33; J34; J35; J36; J37; J38; J39; J50.

"K" Items—12½-in. ....$15.00 Doz. Net
K1; K2; K3; K5; K6; K7; K8; K13; K14.

"L" Items—13-in. ....$18.00 Doz. Net
L1; L2; L3; L4; L5; L7; L8; L9; L10; L11; L12.

"M" Items—14-in. ....$21.00 Doz. Net
M1; M2; M3; M4; M5; M7; M8; M10; M19; M40.

"S" Items—15-in. ....$30.00 Doz. Net
S3; S4; S5; S6; S7; S8.

"T" Items—16-in. ....$36.00 Doz. Net
T1; T2.

"X" Items—18½-in. ....$45.00 Doz. Net
X1; X2.

"R-100" Planter Items....$1.50 Doz. Net
R101; R103; R105.

"R-200" Planter Items....$2.50 Doz. Net
R201; R202; R203; R204; R206; R207; R208; R210; R211.

"R-300" Planter Items....$3.00 Doz. Net
R303; R307; R309; R310; R311.

"P" Items	Doz.
P 1—Low Marmite 4½-in.	$2.16
P 2—Sugar, no cover	2.16
P 2—Sugar with cover	3.00
P 3—Creamer	2.10
P 4—Open Water Jug	6.60
P 6—Coffee Server	9.00
P 7—Batter Jug	10.50
P11—7-oz. Mug	1.50
P12—10-oz. Mug	2.04
P17—Syrup Pitcher	3.24
P19—Cup, Coffee	2.10
P20—Saucer, Coffee	1.50
P21—Range Jar	3.00
P22—Salt	2.10
P23—Pepper	2.10
P24—Cookie Jar	7.20
P25—5-in. Mixing Bowl	1.20
P26—6-in. Mixing Bowl	1.50
P27—7-in. Mixing Bowl	2.40
P28—8-in. Mixing Bowl	3.00
P29—9-in. Mixing Bowl	3.90

FINISHES

All items may be had in the following finishes:

1—Parisian White
3—Sea Spray Green
6—Cadet Blue
7—Daffodil Yellow
9—Burgundy Red
10—Cameo (Peach)

Items J—K—L—M—S—T and X may also be had in:

15—White Antique
16—Green Antique

A 20% additional charge is necessary on: Items A, B, C, D, E, F, G and H—in No. 15 and No. 16 Finishes.

THE STAPLE LINE OF POTTERY

The 1942 catalog featured the last of the RumRill pieces that were made. The new finishes, Two Tone Brown and Neptune Green, were introduced.

ILLUSTRATED on the following pages are the new RumRill lines of art and specialty pottery for 1942. Also listed are the attractive prices, and a new conception of merchandising in the pottery industry.

Ever since our first year in business, our production volume has constantly increased. We believe this steady growth has been built by strict adherence to a sales policy based on sound business. This policy insists upon . . . established price values . . . artistically and practically shaped articles . . . colors and finishes in tune with the mode-creative-advanced and popular . . . products of highest quality which can be produced only by the better materials shaped by the skilled hands of master pottery craftsmen . . . prompt service and attention to details . . . and sales plans that assist our customers in building bigger profits through increased volume and faster turnover.

To complete this plan of individualized sales-service we now offer "private brand" merchandise. On orders totaling more than $150 we will affix your own labels at no increase in price.

Study this plan carefully and compare it with any other from the standpoint of quality, design and profit to you. Then place your order today.

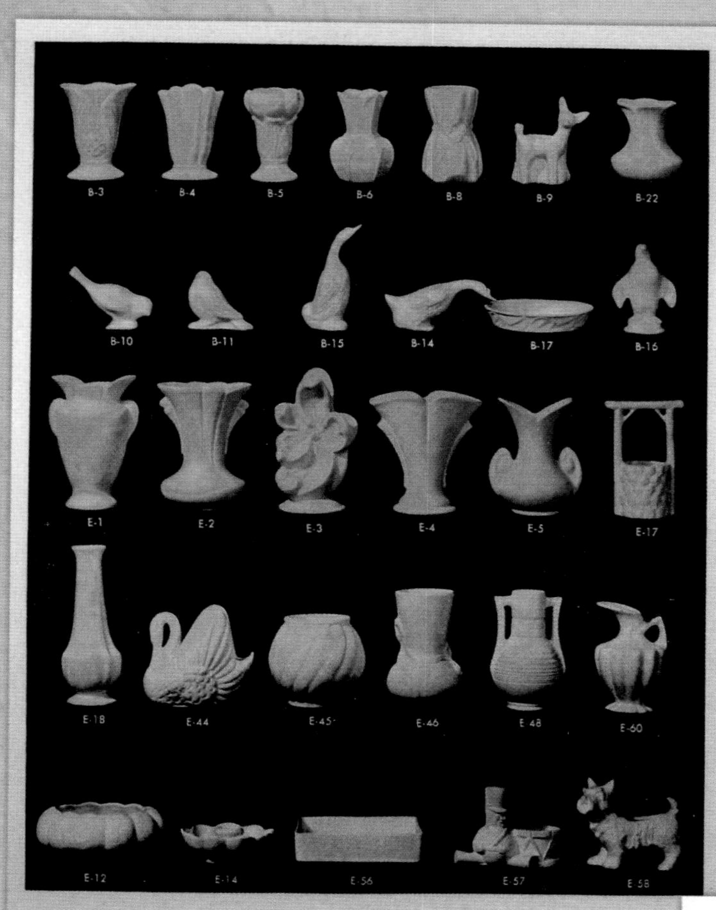
B-3
B-4
B-5
B-6
B-8
B-9
B-22
B-10
B-11
B-15
B-14
B-17
B-16
E-1
E-2
E-3
E-4
E-5
E-17
E-18
E-44
E-45
E-46
E-48
E-60
E-12
E-14
E-56
E-57
E-58

E-49
E-64
F-7
F-18
F-27
F-1
F-8
F-23
F-25
F-26
F-24
G-1
G-2
G-5
H-4
H-5
H-7
H-10
H-11
H-12
H-14

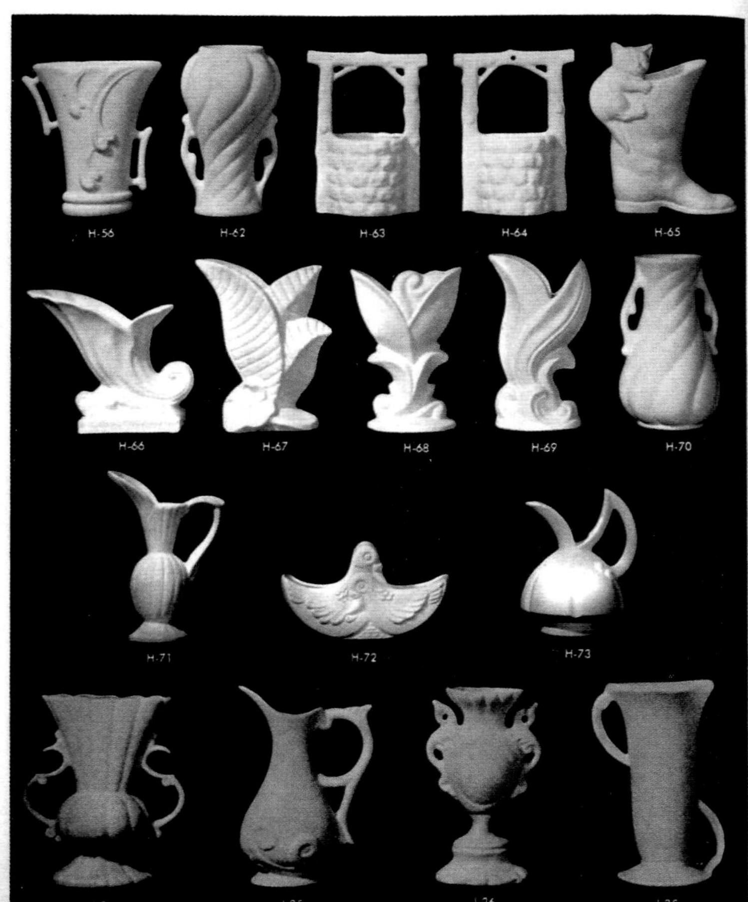

1942 RumRill catalog.

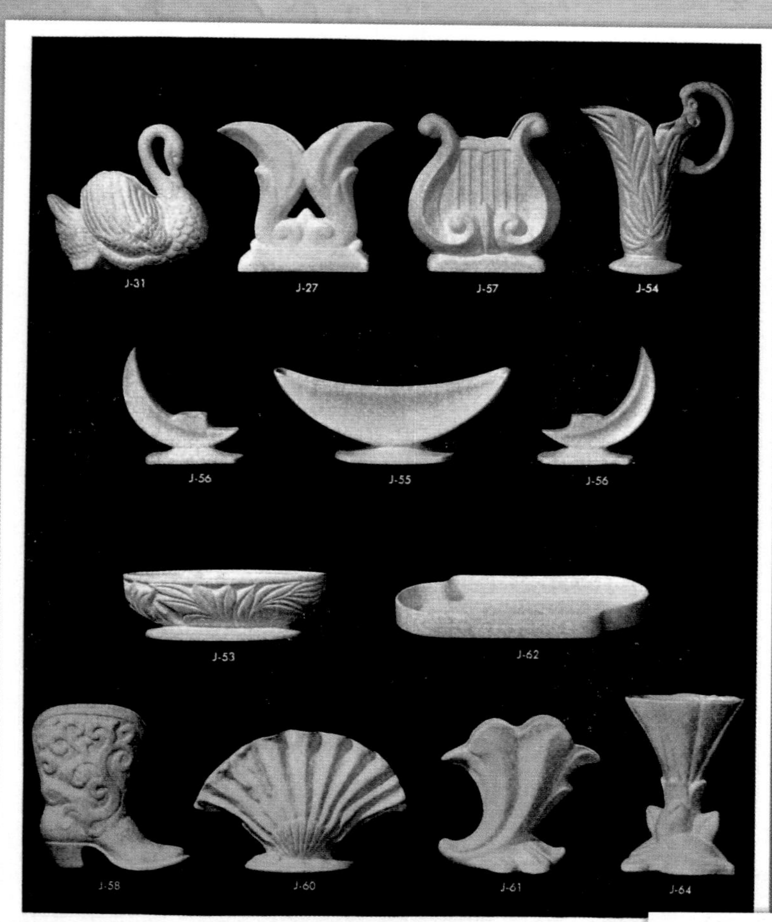
J-31
J-27
J-57
J-54
J-56
J-55
J-56
J-53
J-62
J-58
J-60
J-61
J-64

J-59
K-6
K-3
J-6
F-9
H-21
E-21
E-61
B-7
P-24
P-25
P-26
P-27
P-28
P-29

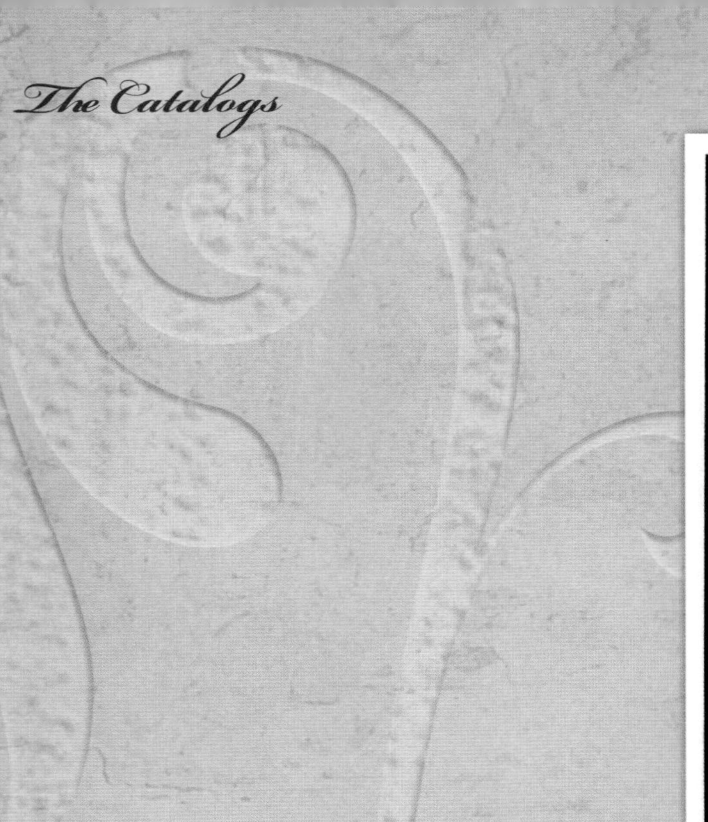

K-7
K-14
K-15
K-5
L-14
K-8
L-11
L-15

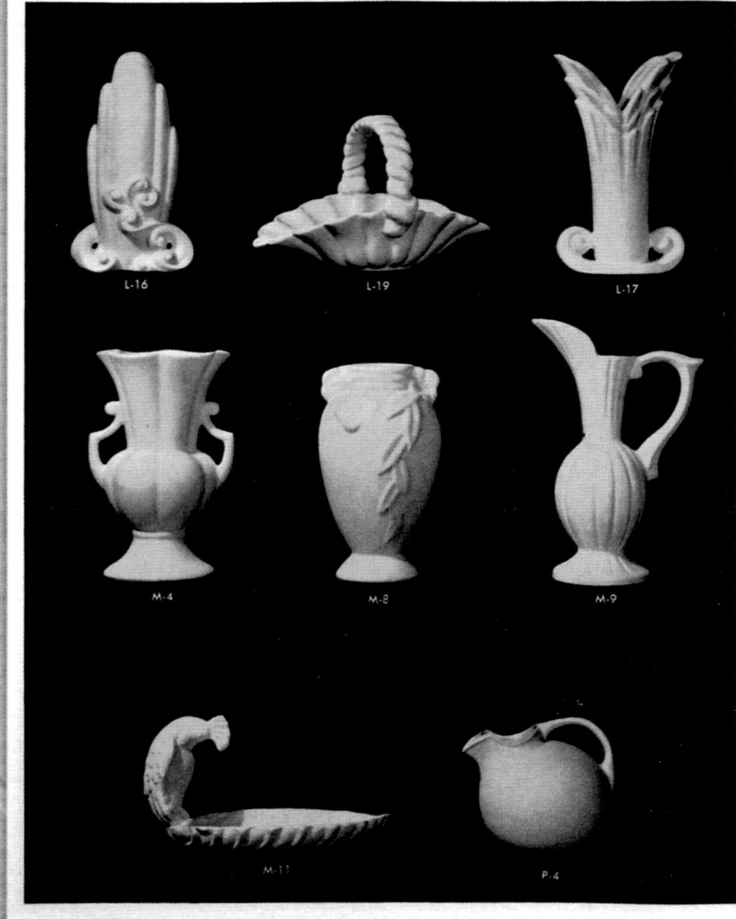
L-16
L-19
L-17
M-4
M-8
M-9
M-11
P-4

1942 RumRill catalog.

1942 RumRill catalog.

501
516

517
505

1942 RumRill catalog.

RumRill Art Pottery

RumRill Pottery Company

LITTLE ROCK, ARKANSAS

READ CAREFULLY

All shipments F.O.B. Zanesville, Ohio.

No allowance for transportation, drayage or storage.

A packing charge will be added to orders for less than $25.00.

BREAKAGE

Absolutely no allowance for breakage in transit. We employ only professional packers, and, in harmony with the policy of all crockery houses in the United States, we do not assume responsibility for breakage which occurs in transit. The railroad company assumes this responsibility and you can collect from them by pursuing the following course:

Call inspector or freight agent to inspect shipment immediately after unpacking.

Have him make notation of breakage on freight bill.

Send following papers to Railroad Company to support your claim:

Paid freight bill (with notation of breakage signed by freight agent).

Original Bill of Lading.

Original Invoice.

By following the above course you will have no difficulty in making collection.

SHORTAGE

All claims for shortage must be made within 5 days after receipt of merchandise.

Be sure to search packing thoroughly before writing us. Small pieces may easily be thrown out with packing materials.

RETURNED GOODS

We will ABSOLUTELY refuse to accept any goods returned to us unless the customer first secures our permission and agrees to pay the cost of packing, transportation and a 5% handling charge.

ROUTING

Designate whether shipment is to be made by parcel post, express or freight. Otherwise the Company will use its best judgment and will not be responsible for any additional expense incurred. Not responsible for goods delayed in transit.

C.O.D. shipments will not be made unless draft for at least one-third the amount of invoice accompanies the order.

ORDERING

Early ordering is suggested as the wide range of shapes and colors makes it impracticable to carry complete stock at all times. The most careful attention is accorded all orders, whether placed direct with the factory or through our representatives.

PRICE LIST (Subject to Change Without Notice)

POSITIVELY NO SHAPES MADE EXCEPT THOSE ILLUSTRATED IN THIS CATALOG

TO AVOID MISTAKES ORDER BY SHAPE NUMBER AND FINISH NUMBER

For the time being or as long as we can obtain the necessary ingredients to make the following finishes, we offer RumRill regular line in

No. 1—Parisian White No. 6—Cadet Blue
No. 3—Sea Spray Green No. 7—Daffodil Yellow

May also be had in No. 15 White Antique and No. 16 Two Tone Brown for additional 20% in cost.

Item	Approximate Size	Price
B ITEMS	4¾-in.	$2.00 doz. net
E ITEMS	6½-in.	3.30 doz. net
F ITEMS	7½-in.	6.00 doz. net
G ITEMS	7½-in.	6.00 doz. net
H ITEMS	9-in.	6.60 doz. net
J ITEMS	11-in.	13.20 doz. net
K ITEMS	12½-in.	15.00 doz. net
		18.00 doz. net
		24.00 doz. net

oz. net P-27—$2.65 doz. net
oz. net P-28—$3.30 doz. net
oz. net P-29—$4.29 doz. net
oz. net

CLASSICS

RumRill Classic Group may be had in the following finishes only at no advance in prices shown:

No. 15—White Antique
No. 16—Two Tone Brown
No. 17—Neptune Green

500—$60.00 doz. net	509—$54.00 doz. net
501—$18.00 doz. pair net	510—$21.00 doz. net
502—$30.00 doz. pair net	511—$18.00 doz. net
503—$54.00 doz. net	512—$24.00 doz. net
504—$30.00 doz. net	513—$24.00 doz. net
505—$45.00 doz. net	514—$48.00 doz. net
506—$21.00 doz. net	515—$48.00 doz. net
507—$18.00 doz. net	516—$45.00 doz. net
508—$36.00 doz. net	517—$18.00 doz. pair net

Finishes on pottery are obtained through the use of mineral oxides. These mineral oxides, such as tin, iron, zinc, etc., are needed by Uncle Sam for export to the Axis via our Armed possible that it will be necessary before the end of the year to make complete change in t call for any mineral oxides. We are experimenting with this idea in mind.

r order as near as is possible, but if there are any substitutions, it will have to be blamed on re stamps and bonds, so that we may end this war in a hurry and get back to normal.

gs orginate in ARKANSAS, including General Douglas MacArthur and Lieutenant Command-

REMEMBER PEARL HARBOR
AND BUY
WAR STAMPS AND BONDS

1943-44.

PA
Box 252C

Gonder

AMERICA'S OUTSTANDING ART POTTERY

THE GONDER CERAMIC ARTS, INCORPORATED

ZANESVILLE, OHIO

This early 1943 – 1944 Gonder catalog features some of RumRill's last products which were reused and remarketed as Gonder.

Introduction

It is with great pride we present the new styling and glazing treatments introduced in this catalogue.

The Gonder Sovereign Line of vitrified china accessories was developed with colored bodies, which insures uniform coloring. Among its many virtues, the greatest is its high resistance to chipping in comparison with many china bodies now being used.

The styling of our contemporary line has been motivated by an earnest desire to combine utility, style and good craftsmanship in things of today. The work of the designers of this group reflects today's world, —sometimes vigorous, sometimes subdued.

The models of the typed art, such as animals, etc., were executed and designed by outstanding modelers in their special field.

The pieces in the Chinese line being introduced are authentic reproductions of the finest museum type and this is the first time this work has been successfully accomplished by an American manufacturer. The celadons, ming yellow and ming blue glazing treatments used on these Chinese pieces are the results of many years research and development.

PAGE TWO

1943 – 1944 Gonder catalog.

Our Chinese crackle is outstanding in its texture and crystal clearness, with both of which qualities the better of the Chinese pieces have always been identified. Never before has it been possible to obtain these distinct characteristics in Chinese styling at moderate prices. It is the type of art which enhances interior decoration from early period to ultra modern.

The two new glazing treatments, gold lustre and gold antique, are new developments and are unique in the ceramic field. This is the first time a permanent gold lustre finish has been manufactured which will definitely resist the effects of body acid or abrasion. Its lustre will *not* wear off. The antique gold, with its rich brown background, is a masterpiece of research development.

Gonder ware is the art pottery made by skilled craftsmen under the supervision of a personnel with a background of three generations of pottery craftsmanship and experience. It is the sole thought and purpose of these craftsmen to produce art pottery which will be respected and appreciated by those who desire to possess the finer things in styling, craftsmanship and glazing treatments,— personifying the best in ceramic art.

PAGE THREE

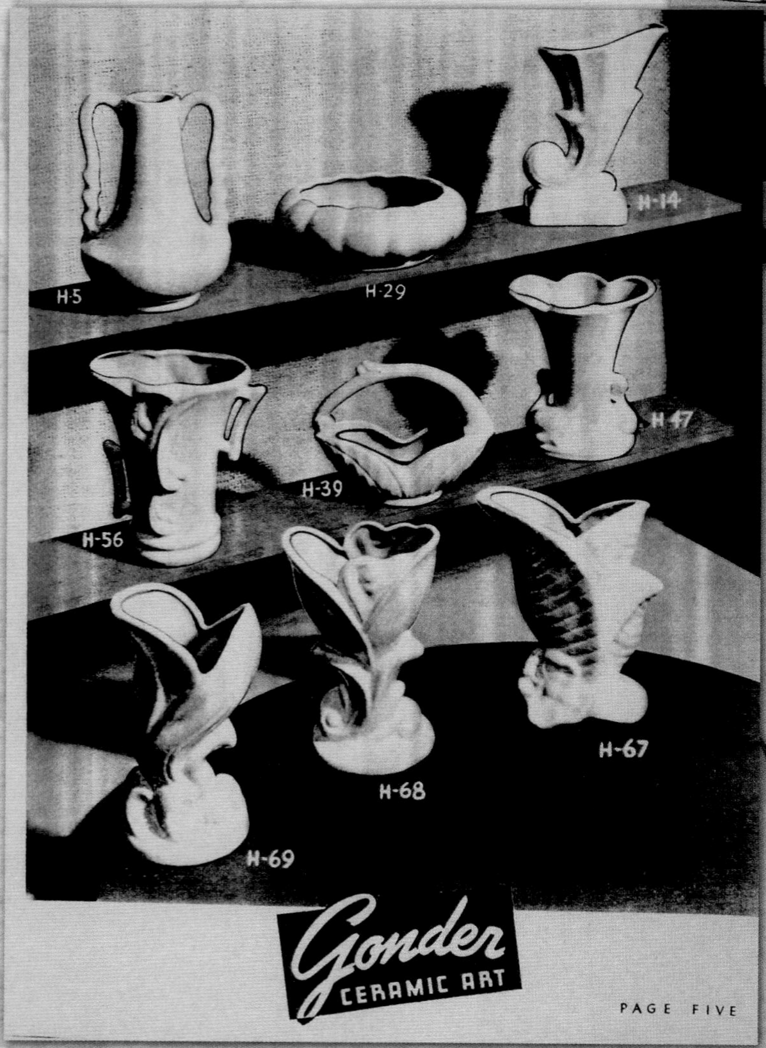

1943 – 1944 Gonder catalog.

PAGE SIX
H-73
H-74
H75
H-78
H-76
H-77
H-79
H-81
H-80
H-82

J-61
J-60
J-25
J-64
J-69
J-35
J-31
J-66
Gonder
CERAMIC ART
PAGE SEVEN

PAGE EIGHT
K-26
K-15
L-19
M-4
M-8
M-9

525
522
503
539
504
521
540
Gonder
CERAMIC ART
PAGE NINE

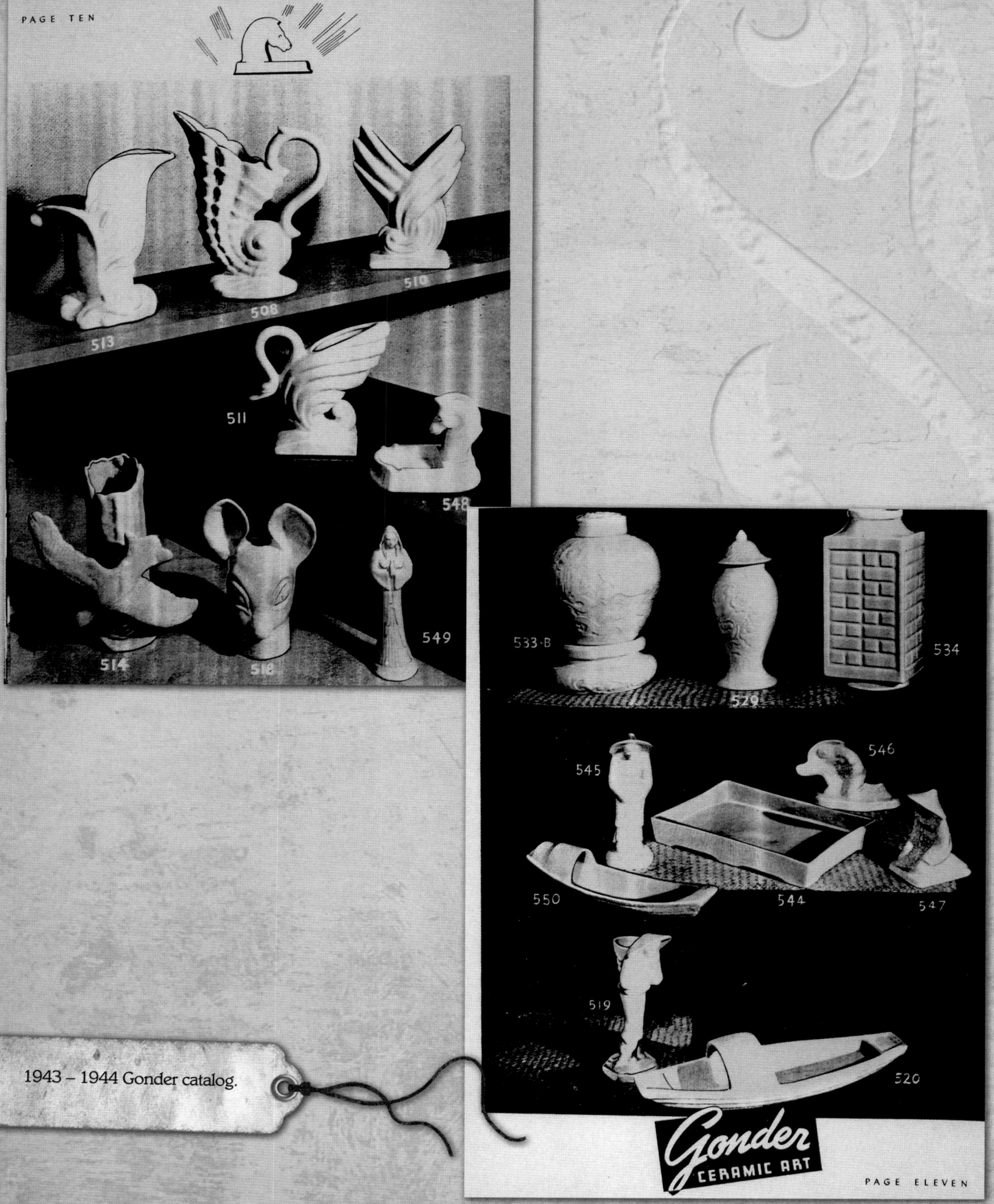

1943 – 1944 Gonder catalog.

PAGE TWELVE

541

531-B

535-B

530-B

527-B

537

551

501

500

501

517

505

517

PAGE THIRTEEN

1943 – 1944 Gonder catalog.

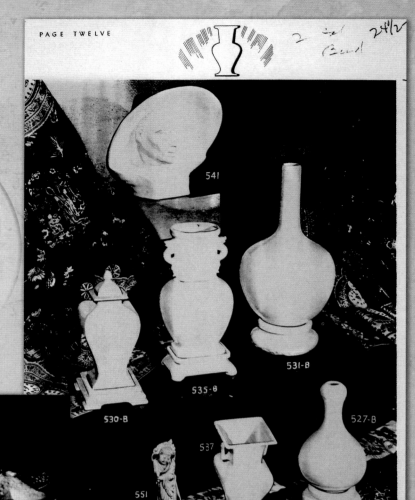

PAGE FOURTEEN

crafted by Gonder factory & studio – ZANESVILLE, OHIO

This label is always an identification of high quality art ware.

PAGE FIFTEEN

THE GONDER CERAMIC ARTS, INCORPORATED

GENERAL OFFICE & FACTORY, ZANESVILLE, OHIO

PERMANENT DISPLAY ROOMS

	NEW YORK	
Suite 641, 225 Fifth Avenue		David Fisk
	BOSTON	
Suite 372, Parker House		Hazel Cormier Willis
	ATLANTA	
Suite 504, Chamber of Commerce Building		A. E. Moncrief & Associates
	FORT WORTH	
1828 Tremont Street		R. A. Best
	SAN FRANCISCO	
278 Post Street		Baker-Smith Co.
	LOS ANGELES	
656 South Los Angeles Street		M. G. Van Auken (Baker-Smith)
	SEATTLE	
Suite 403 Lowman Building		E. R. Wadlington (Baker-Smith)
	PHILADELPHIA	
13th and Callowhill Streets		Rice-Bayersdorfer Co.

Self Feeding Flower Pot

House plants perish because of either too much or not enough watering. Use this self feeding pot with a fibre glass wick that feeds plant from a generous sized reservoir. IDEAL FOR AFRICAN VIOLETS.

Manufactured By

GONDER CERAMIC ARTS

ZANESVILLE, OHIO

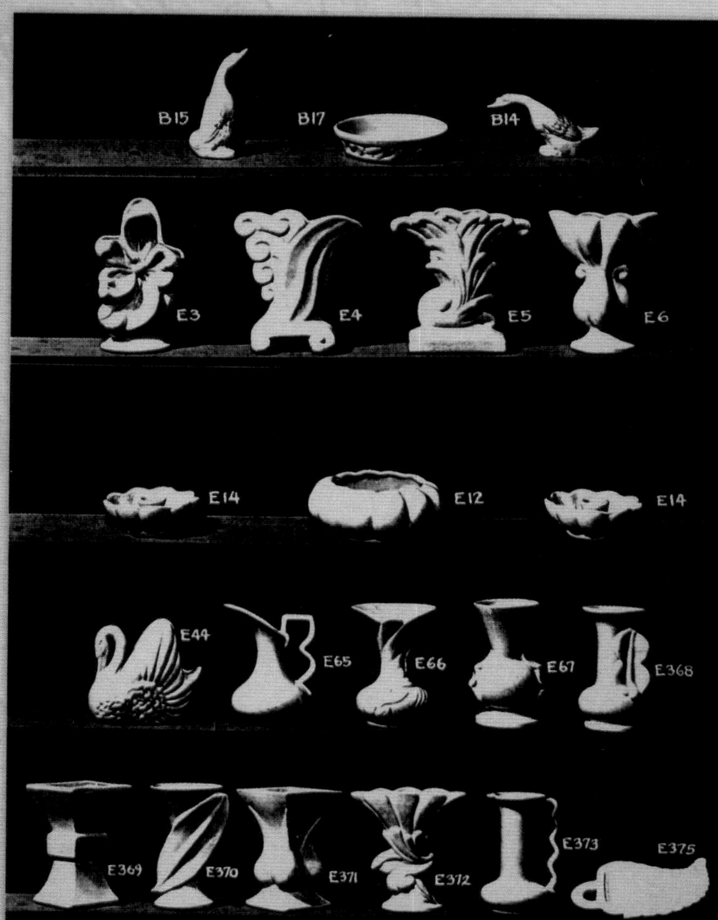

1943 – 1944 Gonder catalog.

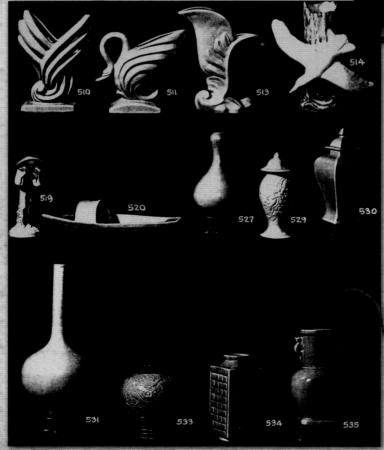

1943 – 1944 Gonder catalog.

BIRD BATH
and
New GONDER "assemble"
Bird Feeder and Planter

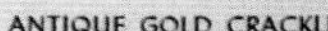

ANTIQUE GOLD CRACKLE

This is the first time in over the two thousand years' history of Ceramic Art that this finish has been produced.

It is obtained by applying pure gold metal on the ware and firing in kilns designed especially for this process.

There will never be two pieces alike. Each piece is individually treated.

Due to the process to which this product is subjected in its manufacture, it is not guaranteed to hold water. It is produced for decorative purposes only.

GONDER
CERAMIC ARTS, INC.
Zanesville, Ohio

Several graceful shapes in Antique Gold Crackle. Buy them singly or in pairs to add the finished touch to your decor.

Antique Gold Crackle is the miracle of modern ceramic artistry. Long a challenge to potters, it had never before been successfully produced.

Gonder pours gleaming 24-karat gold over the glorious symmetry of Gonder shapes, crackles the gold with an exclu...

Each Antique Gold Crackle for... masterpiece, unique, individually ... duplicated. For a striking note in your home, or as a gift, your ... is beautiful Antique Gold Crackle of Zanesville.

PRICE LIST

GONDER STANDARD

GROUP	APPROX. SIZE IN.	DECORATION No. 28 Ebony Green, No. 29 Royal Purple, No. 30 Wine Brown — PER DOZ.	DECORATION No. 24 Mother of Pearl Lustre, No. 25 Shell Pink Lustre, No. 40 Antique Gold, No. 41 Gold Lustre — PER DOZ.	DECORATION No. 26 White Chinese Crackle, No. 27 Turquoise Chinese Crackle — PER DOZ.
B	4¾	$ 4.50	$ 4.50	$ 6.00
E	6½	6.60	6.60	7.80
H	8½	13.20	15.00	18.00
J	11	24.00	24.00	27.00
K	12½	30.00	30.00	36.00
L	13	36.00	36.00	42.00
M	14	42.00	42.00	48.00

WHEN ORDERING please be sure to indicate the group letter as well as the number of the decoration desired. When ordering items in the IMPERIAL line all that is necessary is to indicate the number of the article desired plus the number of the decoration that you desire the item in.

GONDER IMPERIAL

STYLE NO.	APPROX. SIZE IN.	DESCRIPTION	DECORATIONS No. 24 Mother of Pearl Lustre, No. 25 Shell Pink Lustre, No. 40 Antique Gold, No. 41 Gold Lustre — PER DOZ.	DECORATIONS No. 26 Chinese Crackle-White, No. 27 Chinese Crackle-Turquoise — PER DOZ.
500	17½x9½	Shell Bowl	$60.00	$69.00
501	8	Candle Sticks (pr.)	18.00	21.00
503	15	Dolphin Vase	54.00	60.00
504	10¾	Three-leaf Fan Vase	30.00	33.00
505	16½x6½	Shell Console Bowl	45.00	51.00
508	13	Shell Tankard	42.00	48.00
510	11½	Flame Vase	24.00	27.00
511	9½	Modern Swan Vase	24.00	27.00
513	10½	Javanese Vase	24.00	27.00
514	11½	Seagull & Pile Vase	48.00	54.00
517	6	Shell Candlestick (pr.)	18.00	21.00
518	10	Fawn Vase	18.00	......
519	9	Chinese Peasant	15.00	18.00
520	15½	Chinese Sampan	27.00	30.00
521	15	Modern Cat	36.00	42.00
522	9x11½	Scarla Fish	30.00	36.00
523	9½	Butterfly Vase	30.00	36.00
525	11	Game Cock	30.00	36.00
*527	9¼	Chinese Pear Shaped Bottle	18.00	24.00
*527/B	11½	Chinese Pear Shaped Bottle with base	30.00	36.00
*529	9½	Plum Vase with Lid	24.00	30.00
*530	10	Chinese Square Vase with Lid	24.00	30.00
*530/B	12	Chinese Square Vase on Base	36.00	42.00
*531/B	17½	Chinese Bottle on Base	141.00	150.00
*533	7¾	Chinese Garniture Dragon Decoration,	30.00	36.00
*533/B	10¼	Chinese Garniture Dragon Dec. with base	42.00	48.00
*534	10¾	Chinese Square Vase, Broken Block Design	30.00	36.00
*534/B	13¼	Chinese Square Vase, Broken Block Design with base	42.00	48.00
*535	12	Chinese Vase, Dragon Handles	54.00	60.00
*535/B	13¼	Chinese Vase, Dragon Handles, with base	63.00	75.00
*537	8¼	Chinese Square Vase with Handles	18.00	21.00
539	10x5¾	Plume Vase	24.00	27.00
540	10¼	Stallion Head	48.00	60.00
541	10½x11½	Chinese Head	78.00	90.00
544	10x7	Rectangular Low Bowl	18.00	21.00
545	8	Standing Coolie	12.00	15.00
546	5¾x4¼	Bending Coolie	6.60	9.00
547	4¼	Kneeling Coolie	6.60	9.00
548	5½x4½	Stallion Head Ash Tray	15.00	......
549	9	Modern Madonna	12.00	15.00
550	10¾x3	Small Sampan	12.00	15.00
551	7	Chinese Mortal	12.00	15.00

ALL GONDER IMPERIAL PIECES IN 500 SERIES can be furnished in Decorations Nos. 28, 29 and 30 at the same prices as Decoration No. 24.

*These Chinese shapes can be furnished in No. 43, Ming Yellow, No. 44, Celadon Green, at the same price as Decoration No. 24. Decoration No. 45, Ivory White, and Decoration No. 46, Nubian Black, are furnished for Bases only.

GONDER SOVERIGN CHINA

NUMBERS AND PRICE LIST

SHAPE No.		PLAIN	DEC.
800	Doll	$ .55	$ .80
801	Fancy Cigarette Urn	.65	1.10
802	Fluted Cigarette Urn	.60	1.00
803	Plain Cigarette Urn	.60	1.00
804	Cigarette Cup	$ .45	$ .75
805	Vanity Box with Cover	1.25	2.00
806	Cigarette Box with Cover	1.00	1.60
807	Rectangular Ash Tray	.30	.50
808	Round Ash Tray	.30	.50

Suffix "D" denotes Decorated — Color Numbers: White 1, Celadon Green 3, Royal Blue 4, Shell Pink 5, Azure Blue 6. There are two styles of doll decorations D-1 & D-2.

All prices net F.O.B. Factory. 1/10 Net 30 days.

No allowance for transportation, drayage or storage.

The packaging charge is 3%. Orders less than $35.00 6%.

BREAKAGE

Absolutely no allowance for breakage in transit. We employ only professional packers, and, in harmony with the policy of all crockery houses in the United States, we do not assume responsibility for breakage which occurs in transit. The railroad company assumes this responsibility and you can collect from them by pursuing the following course:

Call inspector or freight agent to inspect shipment immediately after unpacking.

Have him make notation of breakage on freight bill.

SHORTAGE

All claims for shortage must be made within 5 days after receipt of merchandise.

Be sure to search packing thoroughly before writing us. Small pieces may easily be thrown out with packing materials.

RETURNED GOODS

We will ABSOLUTELY refuse to accept any goods returned to us unless the customer first secures our permission and agrees to pay the cost of packing, transportation and a 5% handling charge.

ROUTING

Designate whether shipment is to be made by parcel post, express or freight. Otherwise the Company will use its best judgment and will not be responsible for any additional expense incurred. Not responsible for goods delayed in transit.

C.O.D. shipments will not be made unless draft for at least one-third the amount of invoice accompanies the order.

THE GONDER CERAMIC ARTS, INC., ZANESVILLE, OHIO

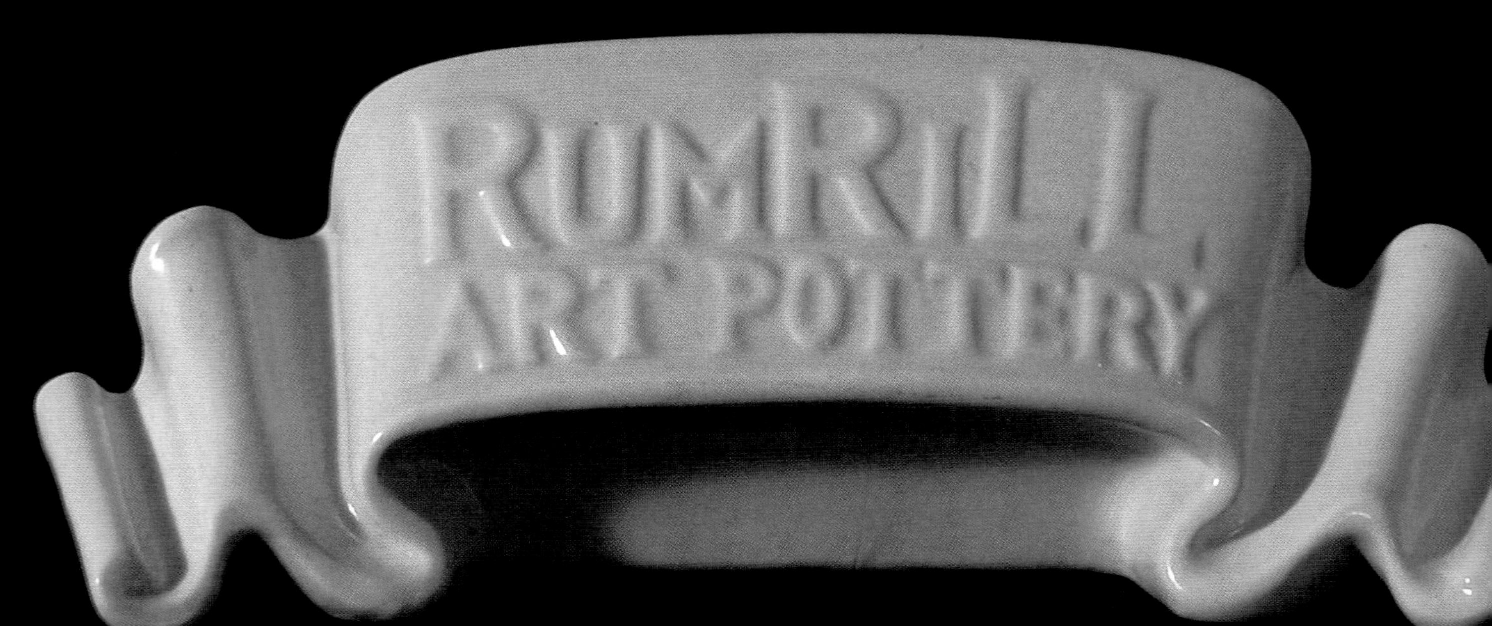
RUMRILL
ART POTTERY

RumRill Stickers

Finding RumRill pottery is becoming increasingly difficult these days. Due to the limited quantity of pieces made from 1932 to 1942, and the amount of new collectors surfacing, there just doesn't seem to be enough to go around. And to find a RumRill with a sticker is even more a rarity considering these pieces are almost 70 years old. A piece to stand the test of time and still have its sticker is surely a prized find.

Various stickers were used to identify manufacturers. Post-Red Wing RumRills can be seen with several different types of stickers.

The most common one was the silver scroll sticker. It has navy blue lettering and the words "MADE IN U.S.A." on the bottom. It was used on RumRill pottery made at the Florence Pottery Company from 1939 to 1942.

This "scroll" sticker was used from 1939 to 1942.

The "scroll" trademark was later incorporated as a dealer sign which is most rare.

Even harder to find is the black and gold RumRill sticker that reads "rumrill MADE IN U.S.A." These pieces were produced at the Shawnee Pottery Company in Zanesville, Ohio. These stickers will be found on pieces in a very matte-looking finish of chartreuse green, lapis blue, a richly colored turquoise, lapis blue stipple, or very light yellow. Most of these pieces will be marked on the bottom with the RumRill mark in lowercase letters with a heavy line above and below the "rumrill" incised mark. These stickers were used for a very short time.

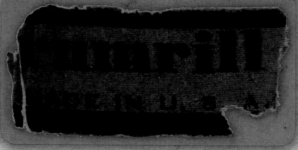

This rare black and gold sticker can be found on RumRills made at Shawnee in 1938.

A second black and gold Shawnee/ RumRill sticker is just as rare. This time, the letters are reversed so that gold letters are on top of a black base.

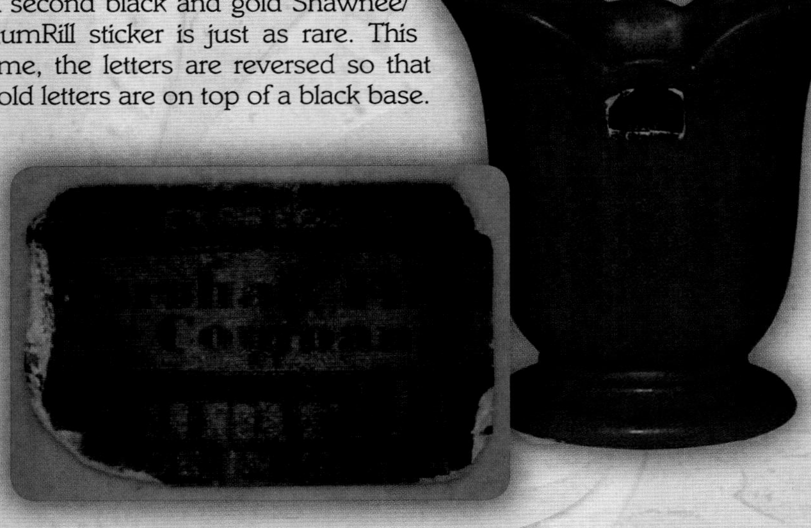

Rumrill offered to affix private brand labels at no additional cost to his larger customers who provided orders totaling $250 or more. This opened up tremendous opportunities with major department stores like Gimbels, Marshall Fields, and others.

Probably around the middle of 1938, the sticker was revised to silver and blue. Pieces with these stickers are usually marked on the bottom with the reverse "r" mark, meaning the lowercase r's are back-to-back.

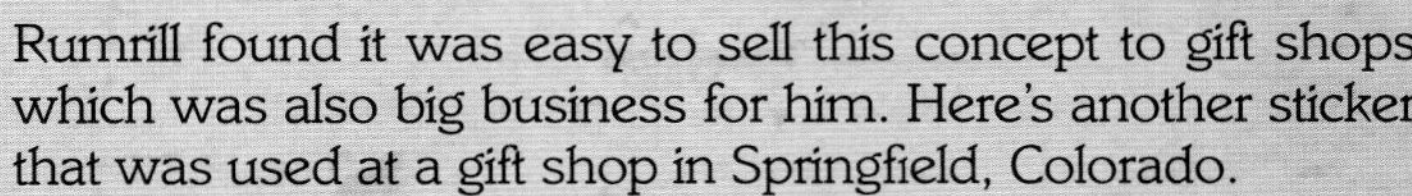

Rumrill found it was easy to sell this concept to gift shops which was also big business for him. Here's another sticker that was used at a gift shop in Springfield, Colorado.

Note how the rounded upper left corner of the sticker resembles a lowercase "r." This was just another ingenious marketing idea that Rumrill did in order to get his brand name noticed and instilled in the minds of the public.

Another hard-to-find sticker is "Niagara Falls." These stickers were placed on small vases that were sold in gift shops as souvenirs at tourist attractions.

Time Frame for Marks and Stickers

October 1937: Rumrill begins to recruit designers to come work for him in anticipation of leaving Red Wing.

January 1938: Red Wing contract is over. Rumrill leaves Red Wing and finds a new maker for his pottery.

April 1938: First transitional period. RumRill is now being produced by the Shawnee Pottery Company. RumRill starts its "R" series. All pottery during this period is marked with an "R" before the letter series, i.e., RA, RB, RC. Black and gold stickers were used during this time.

1938: Bottom marking is a raised block with the name "rumrill" in lowercase letters with a line above and below the "rumrill" name. Smaller pieces were marked with incised, opposing r's. Sometimes hyphens were used to separate the two r's.

Summer 1938: Gold and black stickers are replaced with silver and blue rectangular stickers. These stickers were usually found on smaller pieces that could not be marked on the bottom with the larger raised block mark.

January 1939: Second transitional period. Production shifts to the Florence Pottery Company. Some molds are used by both potteries. RumRill also uses Florence's unmarked planter series and places RumRill stickers on them (silver scroll-like sticker).

RumRill offered private brand labeling at no additional cost to its customers. Below is a very rare example of Strawbridge & Clothier from Philadelphia, Pennsylvania.

Early 1939: Ohio RumRill Nudes debut.

1939 – 1941: Single letter series (silver scroll-like sticker).

March 1940: Assistant sales manager Jack Rumrill (Rumrill's son) sends an advertising flyer with revised shapes. The F-16 vase no longer has the nude on it.

1941: "RumRill MADE IN USA" is kiln-fired on the bottom. This signifies the period in time which RumRill began to export pieces to Canada and was required to mark its wares as such.

1941 – 1942: Fire occurred in October of 1941. Third transitional period. Production shifts to the Zane Pottery Company which later became known as Gonder Ceramic Arts. Backwards (mirror image) mark; some pieces found with a charcoal black bottom. Pieces had flamboyant markings where the tail of the "L" in RumRill was elongated, and turned upwards, or the "RUMRILL" mark would be underlined in two parts.

1942 – 1943: Last year that RumRill was made. RumRill molds were now also being used by Gonder Ceramic Arts. Some pieces were glazed using a shinier finish, such as gray-blue on the outside and pink on the inside, but still incised "RUMRILL" on the bottom. Most of these unusually glazed pieces had a three- or four-digit numbering system on the bottom, also indicating that it was a Gonder-made RumRill.

The RumRill Lines

During the time RumRill made its pottery in Ohio, from 1938 – 1942, several lines were introduced.

RumRill's production shifted from the Shawnee Pottery Company to the Florence Pottery Company in 1939. One of the first lines that RumRill produced at Florence was its Modern Line. It featured the popular Modern Head Vase and Modern Cat for a total of 28 new shapes.

Some of the pieces in this series are marked with a four-digit shape number such as the Modern Head Vase #1001, the Modern Book Ends #1008, and the Modern Cigarette Box #1010.

K-5 · MODERN CAT
K-15 · QUAD CYLINDRICAL VASE
L-6 · MODERN BOWL
L-7 · MODERN HEAD VASE
L-25 · MODERN CANDLESTICKS
RumRill Pottery Company • Little Rock, Arkansas

Crockery and Glass Journal, 1940.

The Modern Line was first advertised in the February 1940 issue of the *Crockery and Glass Journal*. It was a very successful line for RumRill.

The Rock Garden series was incorporated in display advertisements which were seen in various trade journal magazines including the August 1939 issue of the *Crockery and Glass Journal*. Reference to the "Rustic Group" is often used interchangeably.

The Kitchen Group series consisted of bowls, salt and pepper shakers, creamers and sugars, a marmite, syrup pitcher, a batter pitcher, and several other kitchen items. They were dropped in the early part of 1939 but were brought back in August of 1939 due to consumer demand. This is often called the "P" Series.

The self-feeding flowerpot was made in March of 1940 with the first ad appearing in *Crockery and Glass Journal's* April 1940 issue. It had a patented feeder arm. It was designed by Harvey E. Tracey from Fredericksburg, Ohio. There are no known examples that still exist.

During the Spring of 1940, Rumrill stood out from the competition by playing up the fact that he had an "undecorated" line of pottery. At the time, many pottery companies were decorating their ware, but Rumrill chose to keep it simple and practical.

The Sherry-Louise dinnerware line was designed by Louise Bauer, according to an article in the January 1941 issue of *Crockery Glass and Journal*. These rounded-handle cups and pitchers were easy to pick up and set down.

Just introduced by Rumrill Pottery Co. is the new Sherry-Louise dinnerware—in softly toned colors. The shape is simple and pleasing, features rounded handles.

RumRill needed a way that he could stand out from the competition and created a new finish called White Antique. This finish was available, but it was 20% more expensive than regular finishes. In the March, 1941 issue of *Crockery and Glass Journal*, it features a console set and several matching pieces available in White Antique.

Also featured in the March 1941 issue of the *Crockery and Glass Journal* is the first display ad that Rumrill used his new slogan, "The Staple Line of Pottery." This also announced the "summer special" 7-piece beverage set.

Blue, Cameo White, Ash Rose and Mandarin Blue.
For orders of three dozen sets or more the price is $12.00 a dozen sets -- terms 1/15 net 30 days FOB Factory Mt.Gilead Ohio no charge for packing. Extra mugs can be purchased at $1.20 a dozen.
Use the attached order blank below and any orders sent will be appreciated and given prompt attention.
Yours truly,
RUMRILL POTTERY COMPANY
Little Rock Arkansas.

ORDER BLANK
Rumrill Pottery Company
225 Fifth Ave., New York City
Please ship to ______
City and State ______ Dept. ______
( ) dozen 7 piece bev.sets doz. sets $12.00
( ) " 7 ounce mugs doz. 1.20
Ship via ______
Order placed by ______
If wanted each set in individual carton extra cost per set - 14 cents

The 7-piece beverage set flyer and accompanying order form helped to boost lagging summer sales.

Some of the pieces available in 1942 in finish No. 6, Cadet Blue.

Who wouldn't want to sip iced tea from these fantastic Forest Fire glazed pottery mugs? Photo furnished by Mark Ebertowski.

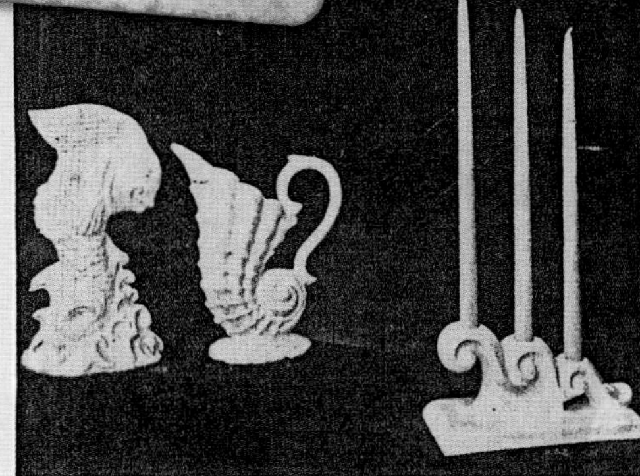

New departure in the line at Rumrill Pottery Co. are these Classic pieces, made in white or a choice of unusual glaze treatment, and moderately priced.

In the April 1942 issue of the *Crockery and Glass Journal*, the fish vase and tankard of the Classics Line are featured. The "unusual glaze treatments" were the talk of the pottery world.

The announcement of the acquisition of Richard Beam's, formerly the vice president of Valerie, Halle Crystals, hand sculptured Crystal Line, made headlines in August 1941. This interesting article came out two months before the fire took the factory. It is interesting to note that not only was RumRill being distributed in the entire U.S. and Canada, but also Mexico, South America, South Africa, and the Hawaiian Islands.

Rumrill Pottery Acquires Handmade Crystal Line

An announcement from George Rumrill of Rumrill Pottery, Little Rock, Ark., details the acquisition of the hand sculptured crystal line of Richard Beam, formerly vice president of "Valerie Halle Crystals".

Richard Beam, who originated in America a new process of glass working learned from an old French glass blower, introduced this type of work a couple of years ago, and its growth and popularity culminated in the combination of the glass workers trained by Mr. Beam with the Rumrill pottery factories at Gilead, Ohio. Rumrill Pottery Co., therefore, are now producers of hand sculptured glass as well as their regular pottery lines. Richard Beam, himself, supervises the manufacture of the glass line which is produced by workers trained by him.

This line will be represented through the same agencies as the Rumrill pottery lines through the United States, Canada, Mexico, South America, South Africa and the Hawaiian Islands.

The Classics Line was heavily promoted in 1942. *Crockery and Glass Journal* highlights the stunning shell console bowl with matching double candlesticks in the June issue of "Right Out of the Kiln," a monthly feature of what's hot.

Richly multi-colored finish is stunning on the bowl and candlesticks from Rumrill Pottery Co., pictured here before the glaze was applied. These are from the Classic line, one of more than twenty different shapes.

CROCKERY AND GLASS JOURNAL for June, 1942

ON THE "ALERT" FOR 1942

★ RUMRILL ART POTTERY ★

plus the new

★ RUMRILL CLASSICS POTTERY ★

A host of new smart shapes in a variety of treatments that are different—over forty numbers to retail for one dollar.

New lines will be displayed at the

PITTSBURGH CHINA & GLASS SHOW

ROOM 691 WILLIAM PENN HOTEL

January 5th, to January 14th, 1942 and all the important gift and trade shows.

RUMRILL POTTERY COMPANY

LITTLE ROCK, ARK.

Remember Pearl Harbor and buy Defense Stamps and Bonds.

The Classics Line was first advertised in the January 1942 issue of the *Crockery and Glass Journal*. The Florence factory had already burned down, but Rumrill kept selling his wares through Gonder's new company. In this issue, the new RumRill Classics line was unveiled.

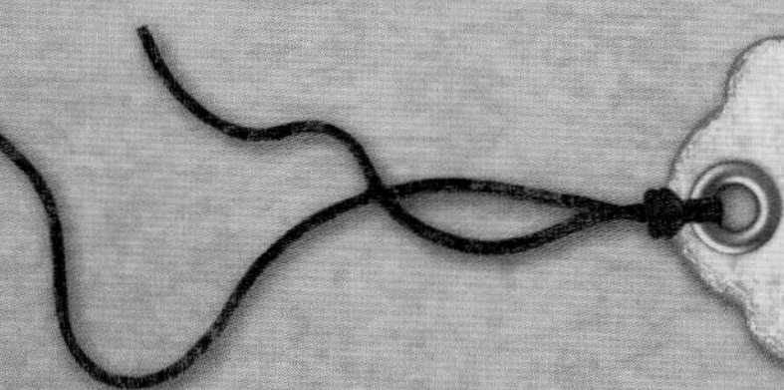

Striking examples from the RumRill Classics Line from 1942. The K-7 vase is featured next to two 512 vases and the 511 Modern Swan. Photo courtesy of Michael Bower.

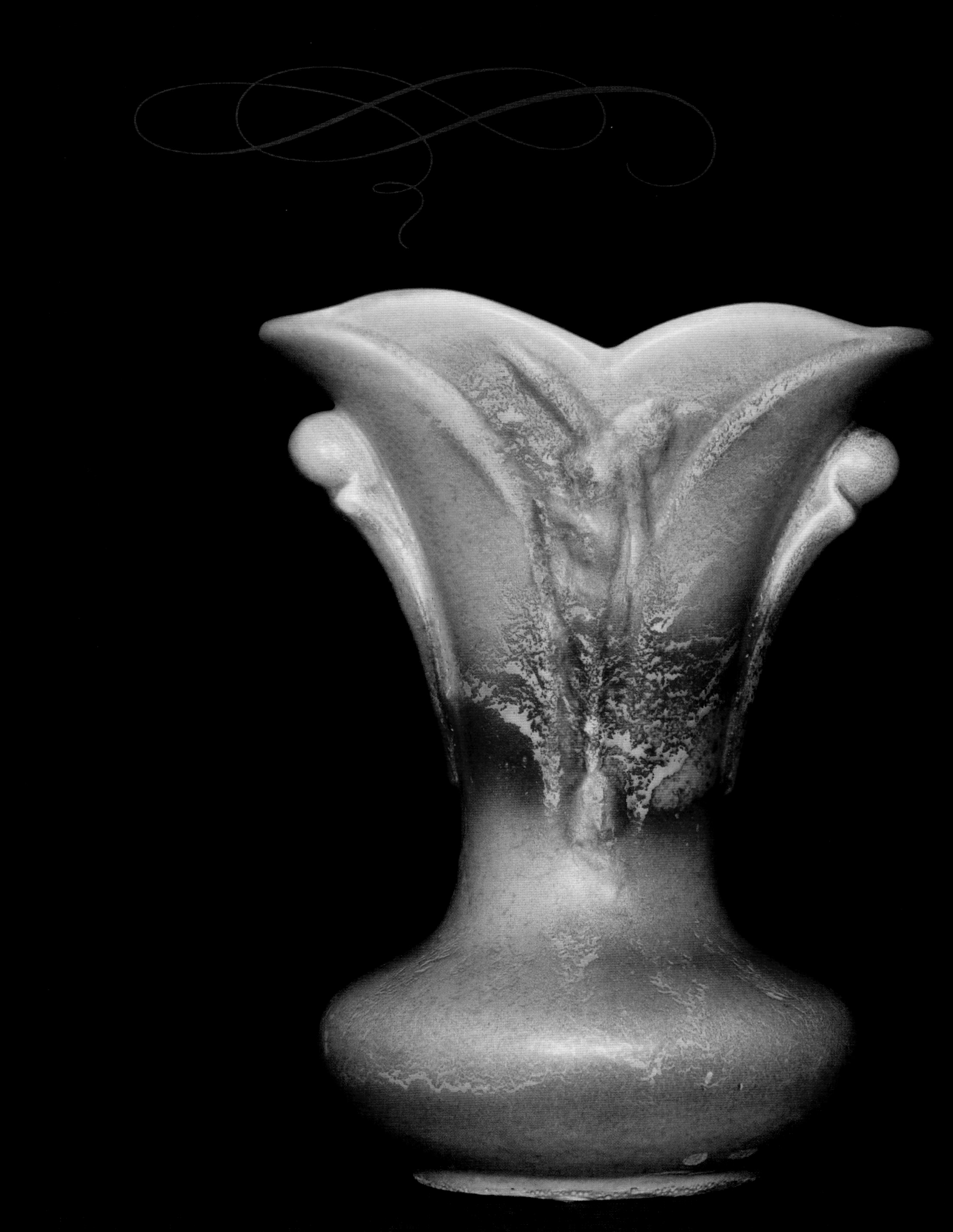

Ohio RumRill Nudes

There are 12 known post-Red Wing nudes that were made during the time RumRill pottery was manufactured in Ohio. They debuted in January of 1939 and about half of them were discontinued by March of 1940.

Ohio RumRill nudes are easy to identify because the nude appears on only one side. The nude will be situated on a raised panel in the front. Each nude is posed the same way: one leg is bent and the other leg is straight, as if she is skipping. The elongated nude candlestick features the nude leaning back with one leg extended in front of her. The smaller pieces, such as the candlesticks, feature the nude kneeling with her arms out in front of her.

Most of the vases, cornucopias, candlesticks, and pitchers are unmarked. There are very few that are fortunate to still have their RumRill stickers on them. Sometimes, the H-25 nude will be marked on the bottom with "H 25" in raised letters.

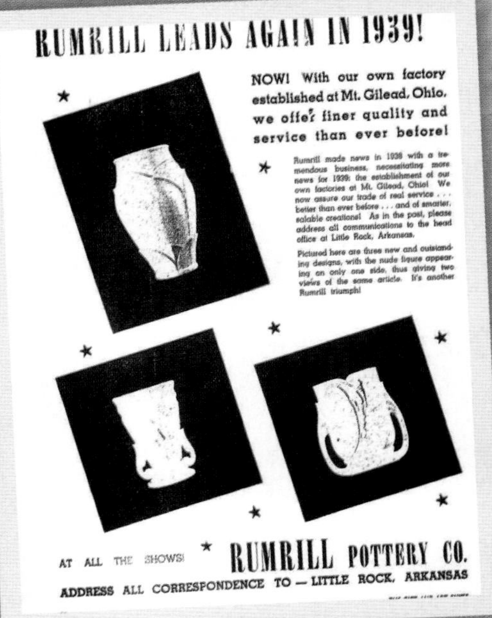

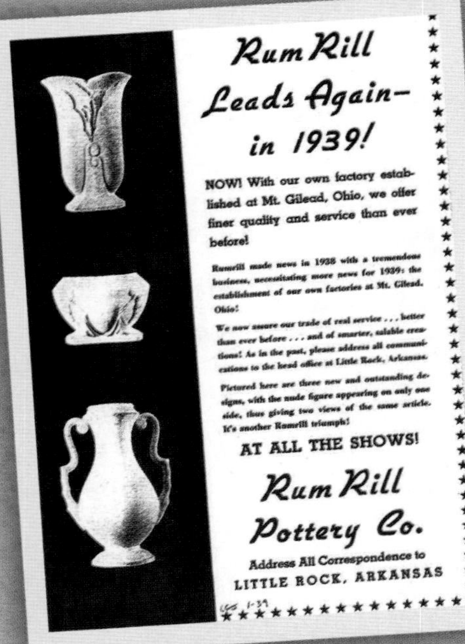

A January 1939 *Crockery and Glass Journal* advertisement reads "the nude figure appearing on one side, thus giving two views of the same article." Apparently, if you were tired of the "nude look," you could flip the vase around to the other side (especially if guests and their young children were coming to your home).

Additionally, *The Gift and Art Buyer* magazine featured a full-page ad announcing the one-sided nude vases. This ad is believed to have come out during the same time, January 1939.

The shape numbers of the nudes are:

- F-16
- F-17
- H-24
- H-25 (sometimes marked on the bottom H 25)
- J-38 that goes with H-57 candlesticks
- J-39 bowl with four nudes that go with H-59 candlesticks
- I-5
- I-6
- I-27
- P-4 pitcher with nude on front

This P-4 pitcher is also incised with the initials "MH" on the bottom. She is a rare beauty that isn't often seen for sale.

Other nudes may have been made, but there is very little reference to them. Although some nudes appear in the 1941 catalog, they are believed to have been offered due to the extra stock that was previously made in anticipation of good sales.

In a letter dated June 2, 1939, written by George Rumrill to Lawton Gonder, Rumrill suggests that the nude group be made in the new antique finish.

RumRill Pottery Company
"Every Piece Built For A Purpose"
LITTLE ROCK
ARKANSAS

Florence Pottery Company
Mt. Gilead, Ohio

Referring to your letter of August 29th, we think it advisable to discontinue the nude group. Isn't it possible to fill in the molds on the following pieces and use as plain pottery.

H 24-H26	H 25 change to F
I 4 -I 6	H 27 change to F
Kl-change to J	K 4 change to J
	J 11 change to I

...finishes. Not necessarily cheap items but a real kitchen service. 5" to 10" mix bowls-kitchen salt and pepper-range set including one, two compartment match holder, one side for good matches and the other for burnt matches-dripping jar-tea pot-cookie jar. We have the mugs and coffee server and water jug. These are volume items and we can get more for a better piece of merchandise.

Of necessity any new plant has to start modeling or an old plant also for that matter.

...truly yours,
RUMRILL POTTERY COMPANY
By Geo D Rumrill
Sales Manager

RumRill Pottery Company
"Every Piece Built For A Purpose"
LITTLE ROCK
ARKANSAS

Mr. Lawton Gonder
Florence Pottery Company
Mount Gilaed, Ohio

We certainly could go to town on the antique finish if we could get it in all of our rustic pieces. Inasmuch as you are spraying some of the finishes, why won't it be possible to make the antique finishes in thie group, and in the nude group only?

spraying some of the finishes, why won't it be possible to make the antique finishes in thie group, and in the nude group only?

Insofar as discontinuing any pieces is concerned, if we do not get the nude group in the antique finish, we will discontinue a big part of them.

Very truly yours,
RUMRILL POTTERY COMPANY
By Geo D Rumrill
Sales Manager

GDR:ma

By the end of August 1939, Rumrill writes Gonder again and agrees that the nude group should be discontinued, but asks if the molds can be filled in and reused. Note that reference is made to "H-24 – H-26" indicating that there might have been another nude such as H-26. His letter also makes reference to an H-27, I-4, K-1, K-4, and J-11; however, these shape numbers do not appear in any catalog. If this letter correctly states the number of nudes produced in 1939, in addition to the ones we have examples of and/or that are featured in catalogs and advertisements, the total number of nudes that may have been produced could be as high as 18 different shape numbers.

In another letter written on October 13, 1939, by George Rumrill to Lawton Gonder, Rumrill asks Gonder to make the I-6 nude with two plain sides. By November 1939, the RumRill nude line was on its way of being phased out.

If you look closely at the page from the 1941 catalog that features the F-17 shape, you can barely see the nude that is featured on the far right side towards the back. This piece was turned around and photographed from the back so that the nude side wouldn't show in the new catalog. The vase beside it, the F-16, which once had a nude on it, was already discontinued by March of 1940 and was redesigned as a plain vase.

Prices for these Ohio nudes vary depending on their scarcity, the finish used, and their condition. You can usually pick up a damaged one for $50.00 – 75.00. Perfect nudes can command a price of up to $250.00, depending on the height of the piece and whether it was a cataloged item. Prior to eBay, Ohio RumRill nudes were selling at shows and antique malls for $250.00 – 350.00 each.

On the following page is a beautiful collection of Ohio RumRill nudes.

Top Row:
F-17 vase, Forest Fire, 7", $175.00 – $225.00.
I-27 vase, Forest Green, 8½", $175.00 – $225.00.
F-16 vase, Daffodil Yellow, 7½", $225.00 – $300.00 (scarce).

Bottom Row:
H-57 candlestick, Daffodil Yellow, 7½", $125.00 – $150.00 each.
I-6 vase, Dubonnet, 7½", $75.00 – $125.00.
H-59 candlesticks, Daffodil Yellow and Dubonnet, 2¾", $40.00 – $60.00 each.

Top Row:
P-4 pitcher, Parisian White, marked "P4MH" on bottom, 7½", $500.00+.
J-38 vase, Gentian Blue, 10", $175.00 – $225.00.
J-39 bowl, Parisian White, 5", $250.00 – $300.00.

Bottom Row:
H-24 vase, Forest Green, 7½", $175.00 – $225.00 (scarce).
I-5 vase, Forest Green, 9½", $175.00 – $225.00.
H-25 vase, Forest Green, marked "H25" on bottom, 7", $175.00 – $225.00.

Identification and Price Guide

When putting a value on Ohio RumRill pottery, several factors have to be taken into consideration, such as the abundance, finish, condition, length of time the piece was made, when it was made, and who made it. As a general rule, the price will be more expensive depending on the size of the piece; the larger the piece, the more it will cost. As an example, back in 1938, floor vases (18½") sold for $45.00 a dozen, whereas the "A" size pieces (4½") sold for $1.50 a dozen.

Identifying by Size

RumRills that were manufactured in Ohio are most easily identified by their height and distinctive glazes. Not all pieces were marked on the bottom with a letter and a shape number. Most markings were either incised or marked with a grease pencil. The letter determined the size of the piece. For example, "A" pieces were the shortest, and "X" pieces were the tallest (although "X" pieces were marked as "T," and "T" pieces were marked as "S"). The number on the bottom was the shape number.

During the course of the four years that RumRill was made in Ohio, many changes were made to the catalogs. According to many letters written by Rumrill to the Florence Pottery Company, Rumrill frequently changed his mind and reassigned shape numbers with a lower letter series. Perhaps he did this in an effort to sell off inventory that was not moving.

You may sometimes find duplicate shape numbers that were issued to two different pieces. Some pieces were discontinued and dropped from the offerings. Some "G" pieces were renamed as "F" pieces, which brought their price down per dozen.

Interestingly, you will find some pieces marked with an "S," but are actually shown in the catalog as a "T." This is also true

"A" pieces were 4½"
"B" pieces were 4¾"
"C" pieces were 5"
"D" pieces were also 5"
"E" pieces were 6½"
"F" pieces were 7½"
"G" pieces were also 7½"
"H" pieces were 9"
"I" pieces were 10¼"
"J" pieces were 11"
"K" pieces were 12½"
"L" pieces were 13"
"M" pieces were 14"
"P" pieces were kitchenware items
"R" pieces were planters
"S" pieces were 15"
"T" pieces were 16"
"X" pieces were 18½"

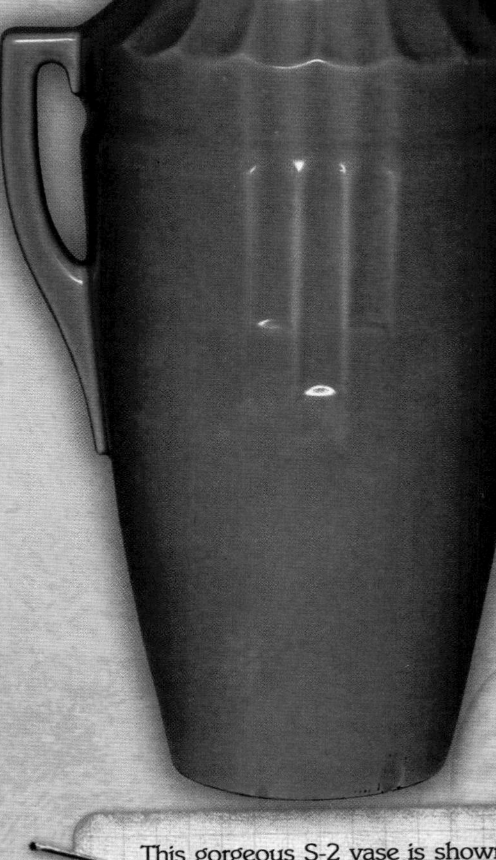

This gorgeous S-2 vase is shown in the catalog as a T-2. It still measures a whopping 15½".

of the floor vases, the largest pieces ever made by RumRill. Although the floor vases are marked as T-1 and T-2, they are shown in the catalog as X-1 and X-2.

Another unexplained example is the K-16 Strawberry Planter which is in the catalog as a J-36. Additionally, the M-8 in the catalog is actually marked L-8 on the actual piece.

You will find some shapes that came in two different sizes: one small, and one larger. For instance, the E-5 vase is the same shape as the H-32 (larger) vase. The D-2 is the same shape as the F-2 (larger) vase. The C-4 is the shorter version of the G-4. The higher the letter, the larger the piece.

Towards the end of the RumRill era in 1942, Gonder produced only the good-selling shapes in finishes that customers wanted. There wasn't a large variety of finishes that were available towards the end. However, 17 new pieces were offered in 1942 and these 500 Series pieces were called the Classics Line. These pieces are marked with numbers only (no shape letters precede the numbers), and they usually have black unglazed bottoms. These pieces are featured at the end of this chapter.

Prices will vary based on the finish that was used as well as other factors such as whether or not a piece has a sticker, and, most of all, its condition. Pristine examples can command the attention of the discriminating buyer. Pieces made in the Forest Fire and Forest Green finishes have a multiplication factor of two times the base price due to their rarity. The finish was hand-applied, and no two pieces are alike.

Additionally, some finishes, such as Stipple Blue, Mandarin Blue, Burgundy Red, Silver Gray, Neptune Green, and White Antique were only used for a short period of time. Pieces in these finishes should be considered scarce.

Uncataloged pieces that are marked "RUMRILL" (or earlier RumRill marks) on the bottom are also considered scarce. Keep in mind that, as with any art pottery, there were lunch-hour pieces that were made by the employees. For instance, one of the larger vases from the Brawley Collection is clearly marked with opposing double r's and incised J-8. However, the J-8 that is featured in the 1941 catalog shows the piece as a large bowl.

Stickered pieces have greater value, especially if the sticker is an early black and gold "rumrill" label. This indicates the early Ohio years.

Some RumRill pottery will be marked on the bottom with either "rr," or reversed or opposing "rr's," "RUMRILL," or "RUMRILL Made in U.S.A." They should also have a letter (indicating the shape) and a number, i.e., "RUMRILL C9." To make it easier on the eyes, we separated the shape from the number with a hyphen. So a C9 piece will be identified in the Price Guide as C-9.

An H-7 vase (left) and its larger version, the L-2.

Some pieces of RumRill will be marked with a double letter, i.e., RH-9. You may also find this same vase marked H-9. These early, double-lettered post-Red Wing pieces that were made at Shawnee are very hard to find and very desirable to collectors. They signify a production period that spans less than a year. These double-lettered vases are generally very matte-looking in appearance, and display more quality than those made at Florence.

When identifying any double-letter RumRill pot, drop the R. So, an RH-9 is actually an H-9 with the only difference being that the RH was made earlier.

The pieces that are the hardest to find are the larger ones such as "L," "M, ""S," "T," "X," and of course, the nudes.

Remember, use this price guide as a "general value." Pottery, like the stock market, has its ups and downs. It is also ruled by supply and demand. When there is a supply in the marketplace and little demand, the price will generally go down. Additionally, having the availability of auction websites have aided collectors in finding pieces that would generally take many years to acquire and many miles to travel. Consequently, pieces that cost $30.00 to $75.00 20 years ago are selling for half that due to them now being readily available online.

I remember being the first one in line at an antiques show ten years ago and I was lucky if I would find one piece of RumRill. Today, all I have to do is cruise the internet and I can find pieces to add to my collection. What has taken a collector 30 years to accomplish can now be achieved within one or two years...as long as you have money to spend and time to hunt. The bottom line is, a piece is only worth what someone is willing to pay. Period.

In the pages to follow, you will see that we attempted to re-create the 1941 catalog in order to aid in identification and pricing. The "A" series contains the shortest pieces and the "T" and "X" pieces are the largest. You can identify your unmarked pieces by measuring them and then flipping through the pages until you find the corresponding letter that matches the height. For instance, "H" pieces are generally around 9" high.

The photos on the following pages are arranged exactly as they appear in the 1941 catalog. Some pieces are numerically out of order in the catalog. Planters and kitchenware were photographed separately.

This particular piece looks just like the J-1 from the 1941 catalog except it does not have any handles. The Ashes of Roses finish is a dead giveaway that it is, no doubt, a RumRill vase, and a gorgeous one at that.

Measurements refer to height unless otherwise noted.
HTF means hard to find.
Scarce means very limited quantities were made.
If the piece has no value next to it, the author and colleagues have not seen one and cannot say with certainty what value to assign.
Pieces that are missing from the collection are noted as **not shown.**

Top Row:
A-1 vase, Dubonnet, 4", $25.00 – 50.00 (scarce).
A-2 vase, Cadet Blue, 4", $30.00 – 40.00 ($15.00 – 20.00 in other finishes).
A-3 vase, Daffodil Yellow, 4", $15.00 – 20.00.
A-5 vase, Cadet Blue, 4", $30.00 – 40.00 ($15.00 – 20.00 in other finishes).
A-6, Forest Green, 4⅛", $15.00 – 20.00.
A-7, not shown, $20.00 – 30.00.
A-8 shoe planter, Sea Spray Green, 2", $15.00 – 20.00.

Bottom Row:
A-9 penguin, Parisian White, 2", $50.00 – 75.00.
A-10 candleholder, Parisian White, 2", $20.00 – 30.00 (HTF).
B-1 ashtray, not shown, $75.00 – 100.00 (scarce).
B-2 vase, Sea Spray Green, 4½", $50.00 – 80.00 (less with a more common finish).
B-3 vase, Dubonnet, 4½", $30.00 – 40.00.
B-4 vase, Forest Green, 5", $35.00 – 50.00 (less with a more common finish).

Top Row:
B-5 vase, Cadet Blue, 4½", $15.00 – 20.00.
B-6 vase, Stipple Blue, 4½", $35.00 – 70.00 (depending on glaze).
B-7 candleholder, not shown, $20.00 – 30.00.
B-8 creamer, Cadet Blue, 2", $15.00 – 20.00.
B-8 sugar, not shown, 2", $15.00 – 20.00.
B-10 bird, Cameo, 3¼", $15.00 – 20.00.
B-11 bird, Cameo, 3", $15.00 – 20.00.

Bottom Row:
B-12 cradle planter, not shown, $20.00 – 30.00 (scarce).
B-13 teddy bear small planter, not shown, $25.00 – 30.00 (scarce).
B-15 bird with head up, not shown, $15.00 – 20.00.
B-14 bird with head down, Cadet Blue, 3", $15.00 – 20.00.
B-16 shoe planter, not shown, $15.00 – 25.00.
B-17 basket, Sea Spray Green, 3½", $25.00 – 30.00.
B-18 vase, not shown, $15.00 – 20.00.
B-20 cup, Stipple Blue, 3¼", $35.00 – 70.00 (scarce).
C-1 vase, Forest Fire, 4", $40.00 – 50.00 (less with a more common finish).

Top Row:
C-2 vase, Dubonnet, 4", $25.00 – 30.00.
C-3 vase, Buttercup Yellow, 4½", $40.00 – 50.00 (less with a more common finish).
C-4 vase, Stipple Blue, 4¼", $35.00 – 50.00 (less with a more common finish).
C-5 vase, Cameo, 4", $25.00 – 30.00.

Bottom Row:
C-8 vase, Forest Fire, 4½", $25.00 – 30.00 (less with a more common finish).
C-7 vase, Stipple Blue, 4¼", $25.00 – 30.00 (less with a more common finish).
C-9 vase, Gentian Blue, 4¾", $25.00 – 30.00.
C-10 vase, Sea Spray Green, 4½", $25.00 – 30.00.

Top Row:
D-21 planter with attached saucer, not shown, $30.00 – 50.00 (scarce).
D-20 planter, Sea Spray Green, 3½", $25.00 – 30.00.
C-19 bowl, not shown.
D-2 vase, Cadet Blue, 5", $25.00 – 30.00.
E-41 with E-42 accompanying saucer, Cameo, 3", $30.00 – 50.00.
E-40 low bowl, not shown.
C-11 salt & pepper shakers, not shown.
E-43 bowl, not shown.
E-21 flowerpot with attached saucer, not shown.
E-38 bowl, not shown.
E-17 miniature ivy bowl (wishing well), Forest Fire, 6", $45.00 – 60.00 (less with a more common finish).

Bottom Row:
D-1 vase, Sea Spray Green, 5¾", $25.00 – 30.00.
D-10 handled basket, Cameo, 6", $25.00 – 30.00.
E-42 saucer (see E-41 for set).
E-39 pig planter, not shown, $35.00 – 50.00 (scarce).
E-50 rock bowl, not shown.
E-44 swan planter, Parisian White, 5", $25.00 – 40.00.
E-1 vase, Gentian Blue, 6½", $35.00 – 50.00.

Top Row:
E-2 vase, Forest Fire, 6½", $50.00 – 65.00 (less with a more common finish).
E-3 vase, experimental glaze, 6¼", $50.00 – 65.00 (less with a more common finish).
E-4 vase, Sea Spray Green, 6¼", $25.00 – 30.00.
E-5 vase, Forest Fire, 6", $35.00 – 50.00 (less with a more common finish).

Bottom Row:
E-11 vase, Stipple Blue, 6", $30.00 – 45.00 (less with a more common finish).
E-20 planter, not shown.
E-18 vase, Sea Spray Green, 8¼", $25.00 – 30.00.
E-46 vase, Cadet Blue, 6½", $25.00 – 30.00.
E-48 vase, not shown, $35.00 – 40.00.
E-45 vase, Sea Spray Green, 5", $25.00 – 30.00.
E-103 candlesticks, not shown (scarce).

Top Row:
E-12 bulb bowl, Cadet Blue, 6" diameter, $10.00 – 15.00 (not in 1941 catalog).
E-13 candlesticks, not shown, $35.00 – 40.00 pr.
E-14 candlestick, Parisian White, 1¾", $15.00 – 20.00.
E-15 ashtray, Cadet Blue, 3½", $15.00 – 20.00.

Bottom Row:
E-10 bulb bowl, Parisian White, 2½", $40.00 – 50.00.
E-19 bowl, Parisian White, 6½" diameter, $25.00 – 30.00.
E-7 log planter, Forest Fire, 6¼" long, $25.00 – 35.00 (less with a more common finish).

Top Row:
F-9 tray, Sea Spray Green, 10½" long, $25.00 – 30.00.
F-10 rectangular planter (stone box), Forest Green, 6½" long, $10.00 – 15.00.

Bottom Row:
F-1 vase, Forest Fire, 8¼", $40.00 – 50.00 (less with a more common finish).
F-2 vase, not shown.
F-3 vase, not shown.
F-4 vase, not shown.
F-5 vase, not shown.
F-6 vase, Cameo, 6½", $25.00 – 40.00 (depending on glaze).
F-7 vase, Dubonnet, 4½", $25.00 – 30.00.

Top Row:
F-8 vase, Sea Spray Green, 6¼", $25.00 – 30.00.
F-16 vase, nude in Daffodil Yellow (nude was later removed), 7½", $225.00 – 300.00.
F-17 vase, nude in Dubonnet (nude was later removed), 7¼", $175.00 – 225.00 (less with a more common finish).

Bottom Row:
F-20 planter, Parisian White, 5½", $25.00 – 30.00.
F-14 basket planter, not shown (scarce).
F-24 vase, Sea Spray Green, 7", $25.00 – 30.00.
F-19 rectangular vase, not shown.
F-21 planter, not shown.
F-18 starfish bowl or ashtray, not shown.
F-22 vase, not shown.
F-110 cornucopia, not shown.
F-13 double candlesticks, Sea Spray Green, 4", $35.00 – 50.00 pair.

Top Row:
F-23 vase, Sea Spray Green, 7", $35.00 – 40.00.
G-1 round vase, Daffodil Yellow, 6½", $35.00 – 40.00.
G-2 vase, Sea Spray Green, 7", $30.00 – 35.00.

Bottom Row:
G-4 vase, Stipple Blue, 7½", $30.00 – 40.00.
G-5 vase, Stipple Blue, 8", $35.00 – 50.00.
G-6 spade dish, not shown.
G-7 clover dish, not shown.
G-8 heart dish, Parisian White, 9" long, $35.00 – 50.00.

Top Row:
G-9 diamond dish, not shown.
H-1 vase, Sea Spray Green, 9", $35.00 – 45.00.
H-2 vase, Forest Fire, 9", $45.00 – 60.00.
H-3 vase, Dubonnet, 8", $75.00 – 90.00.

Bottom Row:
H-4 vase, Cadet Blue, 9", $30.00 – 35.00.
H-5 twist handle vase, Parisian White, 9", $35.00 – 50.00.
H-6 vase, not shown, $35.00 – 50.00.
H-7 vase, Forest Fire, 9", $45.00 – 60.00.

Top Row:
H-8 vase, Gentian Blue, 9", $35.00 – 50.00.
H-9 triple handle vase, Sea Spray Green, 9", $35.00 – 45.00.
H-10 vase, Forest Fire, 9", $50.00 – 60.00 (less with a more common finish).

Bottom Row:
H-11 vase, Stipple Blue, 9", $35.00 – 50.00.
H-12 vase, Cadet Blue, 9", $20.00 – 60.00 (depending on glaze).
H-13 vase, Stipple Blue, 9", $40.00 – 55.00.

Top Row:
H-14 horn of plenty, Cadet Blue, 8", $15.00 – 20.00.
H-15 vase, Daffodil Yellow, 9", $35.00 – 50.00.
H-16 vase, Sea Spray Green, 9", $25.00 – 30.00.

Bottom Row:
H-17 vase, Cadet Blue, 9", $35.00 – 40.00.
H-18 vase, Mandarin Blue, 9", $45.00 – 55.00.
H-23 vase, Forest Green, 9", $45.00 – 60.00 (less with a more common finish).

Top Row:
H-33 vase, Sea Spray Green, 9", $25.00 – 30.00.
H-19 bowl, not shown.
H-35 vase, Cameo, 6¼", $25.00 – 30.00.
H-29 bulb bowl, Burgundy Red, 8½" diameter, $25.00 – 30.00.

Bottom Row:
H-30 hurricane jug lamp, Forest Fire, 8", $45.00 – 50.00 (less with a more common finish).
H-31 bowl, not shown.
H-32 vase, Cadet Blue, 9", $25.00 – 35.00.
H-20 planter, not shown.
H-34 pitcher, Cameo, 9¼", $35.00 – 40.00.

Top Row:
H-21 planter with attached saucer, Cadet Blue, 5¾", $35.00 – 40.00.
H-36 hat planter, Cameo, 6", $25.00 – 35.00.
H-48 ram head cornucopia, Burgundy Red, 8", $90.00 – 110.00.
H-37 rectangular vase, not shown.

Bottom Row:
H-49 vase, Cameo, 8", $25.00 – 30.00.
H-39 basket, Parisian White, 6½", $25.00 – 30.00.
H-57 nude candlestick, Daffodil Yellow, 8", $125.00 – 150.00 each.

Top Row:
H-38 vase, Sea Spray Green, 8", $25.00 – 30.00.
H-44 bowl, not shown.
H-41 console bowl, not shown.
H-45 low bowl, not shown.
H-42 vase, Sea Spray Green, 9", $45.00 – 60.00 (less with a more common finish).
H-46 vase, Cadet Blue, 8", $30.00 – 35.00.

Bottom Row:
H-43 tray, Daffodil Yellow, 10", $30.00 – 40.00.
H-58 (also marked 1018 and H31) cigarette box, Burgundy Red, 2½", $50.00 – 60.00.
H-40 low bowl, not shown.
H-47 swan vase, Cameo, 8½", $30.00 – 35.00.

Top Row:
H-51 vase, Burgundy Red, 7¾", $40.00 – 50.00.
H-52 vase, Cameo, 9½", $35.00 – 40.00.
H-53 chalice vase, not shown (HTF).
H-54 vase, Cadet Blue, 9", $30.00 – 35.00.

Bottom Row:
H-55 vase, Sea Spray Green, 8½", $30.00 – 35.00.
H-56 vase, Sea Spray Green, 8½", $30.00 – 35.00.
I-1 pitcher, Forest Fire, 8½", $50.00 – 65.00 (less with a more common finish).

Top Row:
I-2 wide mouth pitcher, Sea Spray Green, 9¾", $35.00 – 40.00.
I-3 vase, Parisian White, 10", $35.00 – 50.00.
I-5 nude vase, Forest Green, 8½", HTF, $175.00 – 225.00 (less with a more common finish).

Bottom Row:
I-6 nude vase, Parisian White, 7", $75.00 – 125.00.
I-7 well ivy bowl, Forest Fire, 9½", $50.00 – 75.00 (less with a more common finish).

Top Row:
I-14 vase, Mandarin Blue, 11", $40.00 – 45.00.
I-8 well ivy bowl wall pocket, Forest Green, 9", $40.00 – 55.00 (less with a more common finish).
I-18 handled basket vase, not shown (HTF).
I-26 pitcher, White Antique, 10", $45.00 – 60.00.

Bottom Row:
I-24 vase, Forest Fire, 10", $50.00 – 65.00 (less with a more common finish).
I-45 planter, not shown (HTF).
I-23 vase, not shown (scarce).
I-27 nude vase, Forest Green, 9", $175.00 – 225.00 (less with a more common finish)
I-25 console bowl, not shown.
I-9 log center bowl, Forest Fire, 8" long, $30.00 – 45.00 (less with a more common finish).

Top Row:
I-15 console bowl, Cadet Blue, 11" long, $35.00 – 50.00.
I-17 candlesticks, Cadet Blue (go with I-15 bowl), 3", $35.00 – 40.00/pair.
I-12 rock candlesticks, not shown (HTF).
I-11 two-tier rock garden, Parisian White, 4½", $35.00 – 50.00.
I-10 candlesticks, not shown (HTF).

Bottom Row:
I-13 crescent-shaped console bowl, Mandarin Blue, 11¾" long, $50.00 – 75.00.
I-16 crescent candlesticks, Mandarin Blue (go with I-13 bowl), 5¾", $35.00 – 50.00/pair.
J-1 vase, not shown, $175.00 – 200.00 (HTF).

Top Row:
J-2 vase, Cadet Blue, 11", $50.00 – 65.00.
J-3 vase, not shown (HTF).
J-4 vase, Daffodil Yellow, 11", $85.00 – 100.00 (less with a more common finish).
J-5 vase, not shown (scarce).
J-7 vase, not shown.
J-8 bowl, not shown.
J-9 vase, not shown (HTF/scarce).
J-6 bulb bowl, not shown.
J-10 vase, Parisian White, 10", $45.00 – 60.00.
I-40 low bowl, not shown.

Bottom Row:
I-20 planter, Forest Fire, 6½", $125.00 – 150.00 (less with a more common finish).
I-19 low console bowl, not shown.
J-17 vase, Parisian White, 11", $50.00 – 75.00.
J-26 vase, Ashes of Roses, 11¼", $85.00 – 110.00 (less with a more common finish).

Top Row:
J-18 quad cylindrical vase, Parisian White (also marked K-15), 9¼", $45.00 – 60.00.
J-24 vase, Cameo, 11¼", $60.00 – 75.00.
J-25 pitcher, Ashes of Roses, 11½", $50.00 – 65.00.

Bottom Row:
J-15 vase, Dubonnet, 9¼", $45.00 – 60.00.
J-14 basket, not shown (scarce).
J-22 bookends, Cameo, 6¼", $85.00 – 110.00.

Top Row:
J-20 modern planter, Forest Fire, 7½", $175.00 – 200.00 (less with a more common finish) (HTF).
H-59 nude candlestick, Dubonnet, 2¾", $85.00 – 110.00/pair (HTF).
J-19 bowl, Gentian Blue, 10¼" diameter, $65.00 – 75.00.

Bottom Row:
J-16 nut serving bowl, not shown (scarce).
J-23 candlesticks, not shown.
J-36 stump ivy jar (also marked K 16), Forest Green, 8¾", $45.00 – 60.00.
J-34 vase, Cameo, 10", $75.00 – 80.00 (HTF).
J-35 asymmetrical handled vase, Sea Spray Green, 11", $20.00 – 75.00 (depending on glaze).

Top Row:
J-33 vase, not shown (scarce).
J-38 nude vase, Gentian Blue, 10", $175.00 – 225.00.
J-27 vase, Sea Spray Green, 8¾", $50.00 – 65.00.
J-31 large swan planter, White Antique, 8½", $15.00 – 75.00 (depending on glaze).

Bottom Row:
J-37 Deco vase, not shown (scarce).
J-29 pitcher, Dubonnet, 8½", $65.00 – 80.00.
J-39 four nudes bowl, Parisian White, 5¼", $250.00 – 300.00 (HTF).
J-13 box, not shown (scarce).
J-30 rectangular vase, not shown (scarce).
J-50 rock bowl, not shown.
J-32 ginger jar, w/o lid, in experimental finish, 8" with lid, $125.00 – 150.00.

Top Row:
K-2 vase, not shown (HTF).
K-5 turtle vase, White Antique, 10¼", $125.00 – 175.00.
K-8 cornucopia, not shown (HTF).
K-3 vase, Cadet Blue, 12½", $65.00 – 80.00.

Bottom Row:
K-14 console bowl, Cadet Blue, 6¼", $65.00 – 80.00.
K-6 seagull vase, Parisian White, 9", $150.00 – 175.00.

Top Row:

K-7 vase, White Antique, 9", $75.00 – 175.00 (depending on glaze).

K-13 console bowl, Stipple Blue, 7", $100.00 – 150.00 (depending on glaze).

L-12 low bowl, not shown.

L-9 Garden Gate, not shown, $175.00 – 200.00 (HTF).

L-10 shallow bowl, not shown, $75.00 – 100.00.

Bottom Row:

L-1 vase, not shown (HTF).

L-2 vase, not shown, $30.00 – 125.00 (depending on glaze).

L-5 vase, not shown, $125.00 – 175.00.

L-4 vase, Forest Fire, 12", $175.00 – 200.00 (less with a more common finish).

L-3 vase, Forest Fire, 11", $85.00 – 125.00 (less with a more common finish).

L-7 Modern Head Vase, Parisian White, 11", $175.00 – 400.00 (depending on glaze).

L-11 vase, not shown, 11", $75.00 – 125.00.

L-8 vase, Cameo (can also be marked M-8), 11¼", $75.00 – 125.00.

M-1 bulb bowl, not shown.

M-40 low bowl, not shown.

M-19 bowl, Parisian White, 12", $75.00 – 175.00 (depending on glaze).

M-2 vase, not shown (scarce).

M-3 vase, Daffodil Yellow, 13", $150.00 – 200.00 (depending on glaze).
M-4 vase, Cameo, 13", $125.00 – 200.00 (depending on glaze).
M-5 vase, Parisian White, 13", $125.00 – 225.00 (depending on glaze).

M-7 vase, Cadet Blue, 12½", $85.00 – 150.00 (depending on glaze).
M-8 vase, Sea Spray Green, 12", $95.00 – 125.00 (depending on glaze).
M-10 vase, not shown (scarce), 13", $150.00 – 250.00 (depending on glaze).
S-6 epergne, not shown, $500.00+ (scarce).
S-5 vase, Sea Spray Green, 10½", $150.00 – 250.00 (depending on glaze).

S-4 three-tiered rock garden (fountain), Forest Green, 7¾", $125.00 – 200.00 (depending on glaze).

X-1 floor vase, Cadet Blue (marked T 1), 18", $175.00 – 300.00 (depending on glaze).
X-2 floor vase, Cadet Blue (marked T 2), 18¼", $225.00 – 400.00 (depending on glaze) (HTF).

S-7 vase, Cameo, 13¼", $125.00 – 225.00 (depending on glaze).
S-3 cat doorstop, White Antique (can also be marked 521), 12½", $350.00 – 500.00 (depending on glaze).
S-8 vase, not shown (scarce).

T-1 floor vase, Gentian Blue (marked S 1), 15½", $175.00 – 300.00 (depending on glaze).
T-2 floor vase, Sea Spray Green (marked S 2), 15½", $175.00 – 300.00 (depending on glaze).

"R" Series Planters

Top Row:
R-303 Madonna statue, Parisian White, 5½", $30.00 – 50.00.
R-309 vase, not shown.
R-307 basket planter, not shown.
R-311 deer planter, Parisian White, 6", $50.00 – 75.00.
R-206 vase, not shown.
R-207 cornucopia, Cadet Blue, 4½", $15.00 – 20.00.
R-101 pig planter, Parisian White, 2½", $35.00 – 50.00.

Bottom Row:
R-208 crib planter (Florence mold), Pink, 4", $15.00 – 25.00.
R-105 shoe planter, Parisian White, 2½", $15.00 – 20.00.
R-201 bird planter, Sea Spray Green, 5½", $35.00 – 50.00.
R-103 dog planter, Sea Spray Green, 4", $15.00 – 20.00.

Top Row:
R-310 teddy bear planter, Parisian White, 4¼", $15.00 – 20.00.
A-112 bowl, not shown.
R-210 rooster planter, Cadet Blue with accent gold, 4½", $20.00 – 30.00.

Bottom Row:
R-211 squirrel planter, Parisian White, 4", $25.00 – 30.00.
R-204 setter planter, Sea Spray Green, 3½", $25.00 – 30.00.
R-203 goat planter, not shown, $35.00 – 50.00.
R-202 horse planter, not shown, $35.00 – 50.00.

"P" Series Kitchenware

Top Row:
P-3 creamer, Forest Fire, 4", $35.00 – 50.00.
B-8 creamer, Cameo, 2", $15.00 – 20.00.
P-28 nesting bowl, Daffodil Yellow, 8", $20.00 – 30.00.
RP-15 and RP-16 salt and pepper shakers, Cadet Blue, 2¾", $50.00 – 75.00/pair.
P-2 sugar (lid missing), Forest Fire, 2¾", $35.00 – 50.00.

Bottom Row:
P-6 coffee server, Forest Fire (no lid), 7½", $100.00 – 125.00.
RP-15 and RP-16 salt and pepper shakers, Mandarin Blue and Tangerine, with original labels, 2¾", $75.00 – 100.00 /pair.
P-25 nesting bowl, Sea Spray Green, 5", $10.00 – 15.00.
P-4 open water jug, Forest Fire, 8", $55.00 – 225.00 (depending on glaze).

Top Row:
P-24 cookie jar, Cadet Blue, 7", $75.00 – 125.00.
RP-5 ball jug, Parisian White, 6", $125.00 – 200.00 (depending on glaze) (HTF).

Bottom Row:
RP-6 coffee server, Yellow, 7½", $75.00 – 125.00 (depending on glaze).
RP-13 wood handle mug, Mandarin Blue, 4½", 7 oz., $35.00 – 50.00.
RP-11 plain mug, Tangerine, 4½", 7 oz., $35.00 – 40.00.
RP-13 wood handle mug, Yellow, 4½", 7 oz., $35.00 – 50.00.

The following pages show rare items that you won't find too often.

Top Row:
I-17 candlesticks, 3", and I-15 console bowl, 11", Cadet Blue, $70.00 – 90.00 set.

Bottom Row:
H-58 cigarette box, Burgundy Red, 2½", $50.00 – 60.00.
E-15 ashtray, Cadet Blue, 3½", $15.00 – 20.00.
H-22 double-sided ashtray, Stipple Blue, 7½" long, $125.00 – 150.00 (scarce).

Top Row:
J-59 vase, Daffodil Yellow, 11", $75.00 – 125.00 (HTF).
Eagle vase, Parisian White (unmarked), 10", $350.00 – 500.00 (depending on glaze) (scarce).

Bottom Row:
F-25 vase, Parisian White (reversed mark on bottom), 8", $75.00 – 125.00.
Butterfly planter, Parisian White, marked "RUMRILL" (no shape number), 9", $500.00 (scarce).
F-26 shell vase, Parisian White, 8", $75.00 – 100.00.

Top Row:
H-65 cat on the boot vase, Cadet Blue, 9½", $65.00 – 75.00.
Cat planter (unmarked), Cadet Blue, 5", $35.00 – 50.00.

Bottom Row:
B-8 vase, Sea Spray Green, 5", $50.00 – 75.00 (HTF).
RumRill Dealer Sign, Sea Spray Green, 7", $250.00 – 300.00.

Top Row:
J-32 ginger jar, experimental finish, w/o lid, 5½", $125.00 – 150.00.
J-25 pitcher, Bright Turquoise with pink interior (Gonder transitional), 8½", $85.00 – 125.00.
J-61 vase, Gray with pink interior (Gonder transitional), marked "RUMRILL J61" on the bottom, 8½", $85.00 – 125.00.

Bottom Row:
E-3 vase, experimental tan speck finish, 6", $75.00 – 85.00 (HTF).
C-3 vase, bright yellow glazed finish, 4½", $65.00 – 80.00 (HTF).
H-67 vase, glazed Cadet Blue (Gonder transitional), 9", $75.00 – 125.00 (HTF).

E-64 vase, Sea Spray Green, 1942 Gonder-made, 6¼", $85.00 – 110.00.

RE-8, Sea Spray Green, with original black and gold sticker, 1938 Shawnee-made, 7", $85.00 – 110.00.

Top Row:

J-52 vase, Cadet Blue, marked "RUMRILL" on the bottom, 11½", $150.00 – 175.00 (scarce).

J-8 vase, Ashes of Roses, marked "RR J8" on the bottom, 10½", $175.00 – 200.00 (scarce).

H-70 vase, Cadet Blue, stickered RumRill, 1942, 10", $85.00 – 110.00 (HTF).

Bottom Row:

RumRill Scroll Dealer Sign, Parisian White, extremely rare, 3¼", $1,500.00 – 2,000.00.

K-6 seagull vase, Parisian White, 9", $150.00 – 175.00.

E-60 vase, Sea Spray Green, 1942 Gonder-made, 6", $85.00 – 110.00.

Identification and Price Guide

The pieces on these two pages were made in 1942 at Gonder Ceramic Arts, Inc. for RumRill Pottery. They are very limited in production. Some are marked just with their shape numbers. Others will be fully marked with "RUMRILL," the shape number, and "U.S.A." They are most often seen with charcoal black bottoms.

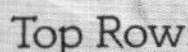

Top Row:
510 flame vase, Neptune Green, 1942 Gonder-made, 11¼", $125.00 – 150.00.
503 dolphin vase, Neptune Green, 1942 Gonder-made, 15½", $350.00 – 500.00.

Bottom Row:
507 pine cone vase, Neptune Green, 1942 Gonder-made, 8", $100.00 – 110.00.
K-7 vase, Neptune Green, 1942 Gonder-made, 9", $85.00 – 125.00.

Top Row:
516 starfish console bowl, Neptune Green, 1942 Gonder-made, 18", $450.00 – 500.00 (scarce).

Bottom Row:
511 Modern Swan Vase, Neptune Green, 1942 Gonder-made, 9½", $85.00 – 110.00.
505 shell console bowl, Neptune Green, 1942 Gonder-made, 16" long, $250.00 – 300.00.

Top Row:
500 shell bowl, Neptune Green, 1942 Gonder-made, 17", $450.00 – 500.00 (scarce).

Bottom Row:
K-14 vase, Neptune Green, 1942 Gonder-made, 6¼", $150.00 – 175.00.

504 three-leaf fan vase, Neptune Green, 1942 Gonder-made, 11", $150.00 – 175.00.

509 double cornucopias, Neptune Green, 1942 Gonder-made, $200.00 – 225.00 each.

RUMRILL

RumRill The Marketer

Rumrill was a master marketer, which was evident in the way the company relied on word-of-mouth advertising. Gertrude Rumrill Sellers, now living in California, in an interview recounted a story about "pottery men going from town to town looking for Rumrill relatives." She described a time when she lived in Minnesota during the 1940s. Her story began with two men knocking on her front door and when she opened it, the men said they were from Rumrill Pottery. They were there to give her a gift because she was (assumed to be) a relative. They said, "anyone with the last name of Rumrill is a relative of George Rumrill, the pottery maker." The gift they gave her was the RumRill Pottery Dealer Sign. She remarked how lovely the piece was and she still has it today. Gertrude said it will be handed down to her children so that the story can be retold generation after generation.

This was actually a brilliant idea George Rumrill instituted in his travels. We know from *Red Wing Art Pottery*, by Ray Reiss, that Harry Rumrill, who was not related to George Rumrill, worked for RumRill Pottery as a salesman after Rumrill left Red Wing. Harry was contacted and recruited in much the same way. George was traveling frequently during the late 1930s and 1940s, setting up accounts with stores, doing trade shows, and just spreading the word about his unique pottery and dinnerware. The first thing he would do when he got in a new town would be to look in the phone book for any Rumrill that lived in that city. In this case, George asked Harry to meet him for a drink and, by the end of the evening, George convinced Harry to come to work for him.

However, the greatest public relations came about with his RumRill Pottery Dealer Sign. Back in the 1930s and 1940s, it was not uncommon for people to entertain at home and to invite many friends over for dinner parties, cocktails, or other social events. Of course, the Dealer Sign became a great conversation piece as well as the story that went along with it. Unconsciously, non-Rumrill relatives, as well as actual relatives, were disciples of George Rumrill and helped "spread the word" about RumRill Pottery to their friends, relatives, neighbors, and business associates. This Dealer Sign story would be retold many times over to other people who, in turn, told more people. Word-of-mouth advertising was, and still is, the most cost-effective way of advertising a company and its products or services. Many of the same business practices and marketing concepts that were used in the 1940s are still used today by many Fortune 500 companies. Rumrill was way ahead of his time in his approach to gaining consumer recognition, customer loyalty, public awareness, and branding.

To further compound his message to vendors, he put together creative marketing materials such as flyers, catalogs, and announcements with attached order forms and postage-paid envelopes. This made it easy for his customers to order his pottery. By keeping in touch with his customers on a regular basis, he earned repeat business and increased sales.

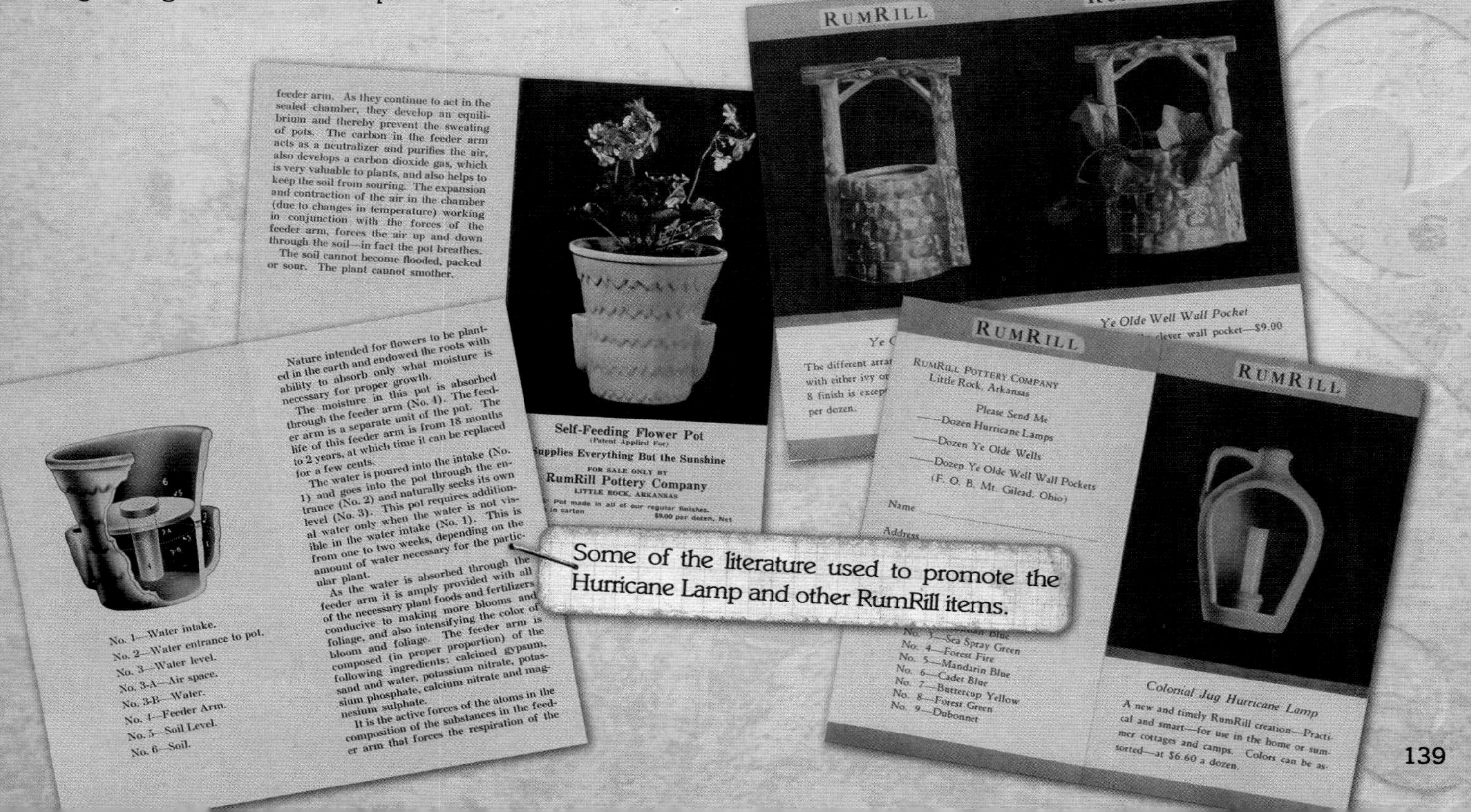

feeder arm. As they continue to act in the sealed chamber, they develop an equilibrium and thereby prevent the sweating of pots. The carbon in the feeder arm acts as a neutralizer and purifies the air, also develops a carbon dioxide gas, which is very valuable to plants, and also helps to keep the soil from souring. The expansion and contraction of the air in the chamber (due to changes in temperature) working in conjunction with the forces of the feeder arm, forces the air up and down through the soil—in fact the pot breathes.

The soil cannot become flooded, packed or sour. The plant cannot smother.

Self-Feeding Flower Pot
(Patent Applied For)
Supplies Everything But the Sunshine
FOR SALE ONLY BY
RumRill Pottery Company
LITTLE ROCK, ARKANSAS
Pot made in all of our regular finishes.
in carton $9.00 per dozen, Net

Nature intended for flowers to be planted in the earth and endowed the roots with ability to absorb only what moisture is necessary for proper growth.

The moisture in this pot is absorbed through the feeder arm (No. 4). The feeder arm is a separate unit of the pot. The life of this feeder arm is from 18 months to 2 years, at which time it can be replaced for a few cents.

The water is poured into the intake (No. 1) and goes into the pot through the entrance (No. 2) and naturally seeks its own level (No. 3). This pot requires additional water only when the water is not visible in the water intake (No. 1). This is from one to two weeks, depending on the amount of water necessary for the particular plant.

As the water is absorbed through the feeder arm it is amply provided with all of the necessary plant foods and fertilizers conducive to making more blooms and foliage, and also intensifying the color of bloom and foliage. The feeder arm is composed (in proper proportion) of the following ingredients: calcined gypsum, sand and water, potassium nitrate, potassium phosphate, calcium nitrate and magnesium sulphate.

It is the active forces of the atoms in the composition of the substances in the feeder arm that forces the respiration of the

No. 1—Water intake.
No. 2—Water entrance to pot.
No. 3—Water level.
No. 3-A—Air space.
No. 3-B—Water.
No. 4—Feeder Arm.
No. 5—Soil Level.
No. 6—Soil.

RUMRILL

RUMRILL

Ye Olde Well Wall Pocket

RUMRILL

RumRill Pottery Company
Little Rock, Arkansas

Please Send Me
——Dozen Hurricane Lamps
——Dozen Ye Olde Wells
——Dozen Ye Olde Well Wall Pockets
(F. O. B. Mt. Gilead, Ohio)

Name
Address

No. 3—Sea Spray Green
No. 4—Forest Fire
No. 5—Mandarin Blue
No. 6—Cadet Blue
No. 7—Buttercup Yellow
No. 8—Forest Green
No. 9—Dubonnet

RUMRILL

Colonial Jug Hurricane Lamp

A new and timely RumRill creation—Practical and smart—for use in the home or summer cottages and camps. Colors can be assorted—at $6.60 a dozen.

Some of the literature used to promote the Hurricane Lamp and other RumRill items.

Synopsis of Crockery and Glass Journal Research, 1940 – 1943

The RumRill Pottery Company was a major advertiser in the 1940s. Display advertisements appeared each month in the *Crockery and Glass Journal*, a trade magazine for glass and pottery buyers, as well as *The Gift and Art Buyer, China, Glass and Lamps* and other trade magazines.

The 1" x 2" display ad could be seen every month. Sometimes a larger ad was used that was either ¼ page to ½ page, which would appear in addition to the smaller ad. The larger ads would announce a new line, or special offers from the company.

In return, the RumRill Pottery Company received frequent, favorable press coverage. Among such notices was one about the hand-sculptured crystal line created by Richard Beam which began in the fall of 1941 and abruptly ended because of frequent breakage during shipping.

Other notices included road trips by eastern sales manager David Fisk, George Rumrill's head salesman. Another press release featured the special Sherry-Louise Dinnerware line designed by Louise Bauer. The usual staff additions, notices of upcoming shows in which RumRill Pottery would be exhibited, international expansion, and other newsworthy items could be seen practically every other month.

One important section of the *Crockery and Glass Journal* featured a monthly news section called "Right Out of the Kiln." Rumrill pottery was often featured, as well as Abingdon Pottery, RumRill's competition. Many of RumRill's not yet cataloged or "just released" items would be featured.

Every facet of the company's growth was documented and reported to the industry. These press releases included color finish additions, new lines being introduced, staff changes, road-trips, public notices, holiday wishes, and even "thank you's."

The RumRill Pottery Company used the same small display ad consistently for three years in order to promote the pottery line. This "repeat message" was instilled in the minds of buyers and laid the foundation for RumRill's brand name recognition. Then, in February of 1941, a new display ad appeared which began advertising the art pottery, kitchenware, and dinnerware lines.

RUMRILL POTTERY CO.
LITTLE ROCK ARK.
ART POTTERY—KITCHENWARE—DINNERWARE
New York Showroom Suite 410
225 Fifth Avenue, New York City
Phone: MUrray Hill 5-7974

Here is a chronological time frame of RumRill pottery as reported in the *Crockery and Glass Journals:*

An advertisement in the January 1940 issue of the *Crockery and Glass Journal* states that there are nine pastel finishes available on undecorated RumRill pottery.

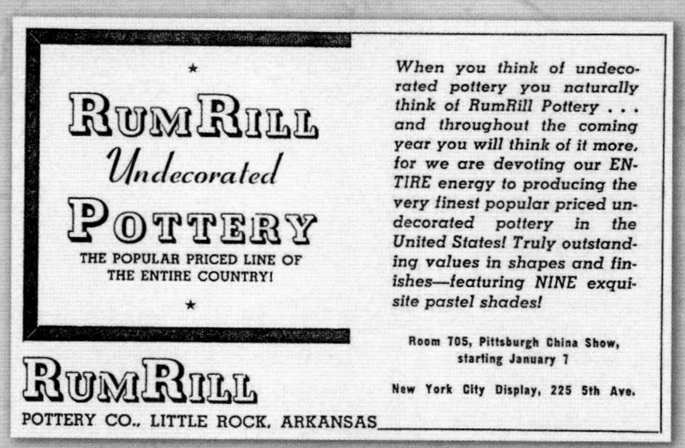

In the January 1940 issue of the *Crockery and Glass Journal,* an exhibitors' list for the 60th Annual Show in Pittsburgh, Pennsylvania, held in the Grand Ballroom at the William Penn Hotel, mentions the RumRill Pottery Company as an exhibitor at the event which started on January 7, 1940.

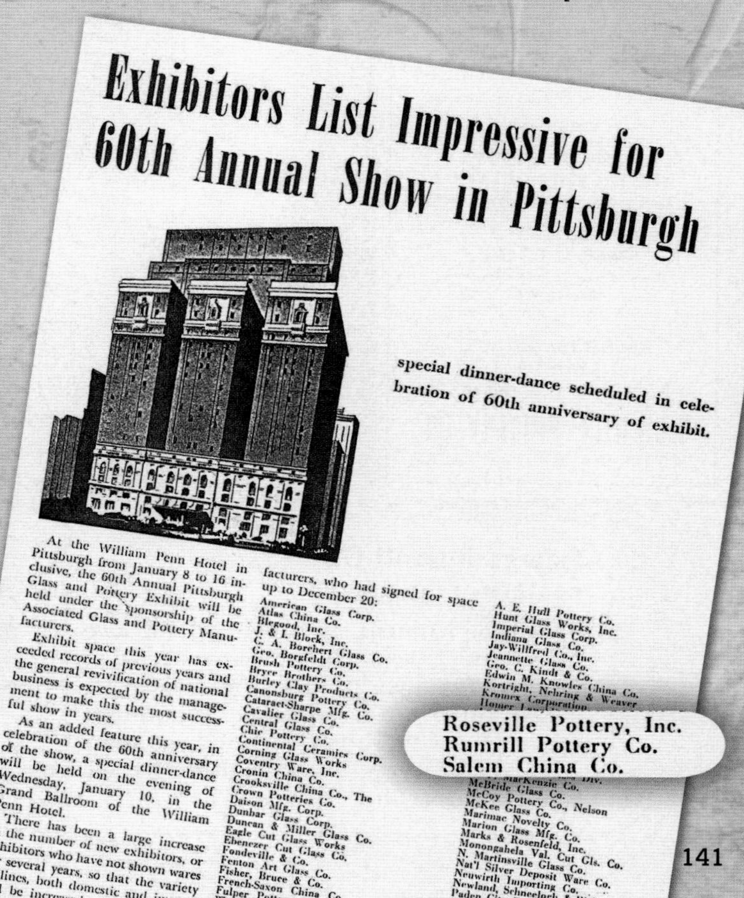

Exhibitors List Impressive for 60th Annual Show in Pittsburgh

special dinner-dance scheduled in celebration of 60th anniversary of exhibit.

At the William Penn Hotel in Pittsburgh from January 8 to 16 inclusive, the 60th Annual Pittsburgh Glass and Pottery Exhibit will be held under the sponsorship of the Associated Glass and Pottery Manufacturers.

Exhibit space this year has exceeded records of previous years and the general revivification of national business is expected by the management to make this the most successful show in years.

As an added feature this year, in celebration of the 60th anniversary of the show, a special dinner-dance will be held on the evening of Wednesday, January 10, in the Grand Ballroom of the William Penn Hotel.

There has been a large increase in the number of new exhibitors, or exhibitors who have not shown wares for several years, so that the variety of lines, both domestic and import, will be increased considerably over recent exhibits.

Following is a list of the manufacturers, who had signed for space up to December 20:

American Glass Corp.
Atlas China Co.
Blegood, Inc.
J. & I. Block, Inc.
C. A. Borchert Glass Co.
Geo. Borgfeldt Corp.
Brush Pottery Co.
Bryce Brothers Co.
Burley Clay Products Co.
Canonsburg Pottery Co.
Cataract-Sharpe Mfg. Co.
Cavalier Glass Co.
Central Glass Co.
Chic Pottery Co.
Continental Ceramics Corp.
Corning Glass Works
Coventry Ware, Inc.
Cronin China Co.
Crooksville China Co., The
Crown Potteries Co.
Daison Mfg. Corp.
Dunbar Glass Corp.
Duncan & Miller Glass Co.
Eagle Cut Glass Works
Ebenezer Cut Glass Co.
Fondeville & Co.
Fenton Art Glass Co.
Fisher, Bruce & Co.
French-Saxon China Co.
Fulper Pottery Co.
W. S. George Pottery Co.

A. E. Hull Pottery Co.
Hunt Glass Works, Inc.
Imperial Glass Corp.
Indiana Glass Co.
Jay-Willfred Co., Inc.
Jeannette Glass Co.
Geo. C. Kindt & Co.
Edwin M. Knowles China Co.
Kortright, Nehring & Weaver
Kromex Corporation

Roseville Pottery, Inc.
Rumrill Pottery Co.
Salem China Co.

McBride Glass Co.
McCoy Pottery Co., Nelson
McKee Glass Co.
Marimac Novelty Co.
Marion Glass Mfg. Co.
Marks & Rosenfeld, Inc.
Monongahela Val. Cut Gls. Co.
N. Martinsville Glass Co.
Nat'l Silver Deposit Ware Co.
Neuwirth Importing Co.
Newland, Schneeloch & Piek
Paden City Glass Mfg. Co.
Paden City Pottery Co.

Synopsis of Crockery and Glass Journal Research, 1940 – 1943

In the February 1940 issue of the *Crockery and Glass Journal,* RumRill introduces new shapes in pastel colors.

4. Vase, pitcher and small well are from the new line of art pottery at RumRill Pottery Co. Done in pastel colors or white, the two large pieces retail for $1 each, the well for 50c.

In the March 1940 issue, RumRill Pottery advertises its catchy slogan: "Every piece built with a purpose."

RUMRILL POTTERY

See the leading undecorated line of Art Pottery in the country. Rumrill means smart styles, new colors and long profits.

Over two hundred shapes in ten color treatments — over sixty items to retail at one dollar.

and NOW!

NEW RUMRILL AMERICAN ART GLASS—

Introducing a brand new line of hand made decorative glassware—in a profusion of new shapes using an entirely new color process.

plus

RUMRILL WOOD PRODUCTS—

Distinctly new and smart novelties that are different.

NEW LINES WILL BE DISPLAYED
NEW YORK CHINA & GLASS SHOW
Room 930 Hotel Vanderbilt July 7-13

•

PHILADELPHIA GIFT SHOW
Room 457 Benjamin Franklin Hotel
Aug. 19 to 23

•

PERMANENT NEW YORK DISPLAY
SUITE 410
225 Fifth Ave. New York City

RUMRILL POTTERY CO.
LITTLE ROCK, ARK.

An advertisement in the July 1940 issue states that there are ten finishes. This large, half-page ad also announces the wood products and art glass line.

In a March 1941 press release, Rumrill mentions his travels and lets the public know he is a man on the go!

George Rumrill On Eastern Trip

George Rumrill, president of the Rumrill Pottery Co., has been visiting the New York office of his firm and is making a three to four week trip through the eastern territories, including attendance at the New York and Boston Gift Shows.

In a November 1941 advertisement, RumRill apologizes for the inconvenience that the fire has caused and assures its customers that its wares will be on display at the shows in 1942.

TO OUR FRIENDS AND CUSTOMERS

We sincerely regret the inconvenience that the fire at our factory has caused you. This fire has prevented shipment of many of your orders.

We very much appreciate the business which you have given us in the past.

RUMRILL POTTERY for 1942 will be on display at all the shows.

Our best wishes for a successful Fall season—and A Merry Christmas and a Happy and Prosperous New Year.

THE RUMRILL POTTERY COMPANY
George D. Rumrill—President
LITTLE ROCK ARKANSAS

In the January 1942 issue an announcement is made concerning the formation of Gonder Ceramic Arts, Inc.

New Firm Formed

The formation of The Gonder Ceramic Arts, Inc., Zanesville, Ohio, has been announced with Frank J. Collopy, Imogene L. James and Charles J. McGreevey as incorporators. According to reports, Lawton Gonder, superintendent of the Florence Pottery Co., which was destroyed by fire in October, will take charge of the new pottery.

The "Traveler's Time Table" section in October 1942 mentioned Mr. David Fisk, who represented the RumRill Pottery Company.

RUMRILL POTTERY CO.

Mr. David Fisk

Oct. 11-12-13
Washington, D. C.
Hotel Harrington

Oct. 14-15
Baltimore, Md.
Lord Baltimore Hotel

Oct. 19-20
Harrisburg, Pa.
Penn Harris Hotel

Oct. 25-26-27
Pittsburgh, Pa.
William Penn Hotel

Nov. 1-2-3
Buffalo, N. Y.
Hotel Statler

Nov. 4-5
Rochester, N. Y.
Hotel Seneca

Nov. 6-7
Syracuse, N. Y.
Hotel Onandoga

In the January 1943 issue of the *Crockery and Glass Journal*, David Fisk is mentioned as the eastern sales manager for Gonder Ceramic Arts, Inc.

David Fisk with Gonder

David Fisk, for many years prominent in the china importing business and in recent years eastern sales manager for Rumrill Pottery, has become eastern sales manager for Gonder Ceramic Arts, Inc. Mr. Fisk will cover the same territories with the Gonder line as previously with the Rumrill line. His New York headquarters are at 225 Fifth Avenue.

Also appearing in this same issue is a photo of Lawton W. Gonder who is stated to be "formerly engaged largely in the manufacture of special mould work for a prominent art pottery organization, has severed its connection with that firm; it will henceforth devote all its plant facilities to an artware line to be merchandised under its own name."

Gonder Ceramic Arts Producing Line Under Own Name; Severs Special Mould Contract

Gonder Ceramic Arts, Inc., of Zanesville, Ohio, formerly engaged largely in the manufacture of special mould work for a prominent art pottery organization, has severed its connection with that firm; it will henceforth devote all its plant facilities to an artware line to be merchandised under its own name.

Mr. Lawton Gonder is the prime mover in the organization.

Rose Friedman Joins Lilienthal

Rose L. Friedman has been assigned to the china, glass, gift and lamp departments at Felix Lilienthal & Co., Inc., New York, it is reported. Miss Friedman joins Lilienthal after a seven year connection with the firm of Edward P. Paul & Co. of New York.

New Pottery Makes Giftwares

A new pottery operating under the name of The Wilmar Co. at 247 S. Third St., Philadelphia, Pa., is now manufacturing a line of china giftware items, which include, cigarette boxes, vases, small hurricane lamps (not electric), urns, candlesticks, etc. The pottery is under the management of Morris and William Greenspan.

Lawton W. Gonder

CROCKERY & GLASS JOURNAL for January, 1943

In February 1943, a notice appeared that the RumRill Pottery Plant was closing due to the illness of George Rumrill.

Rumrill Pottery Closes

It has been announced that due to the serious illness of George D. Rumrill, owner of the Rumrill Pottery Co., Little Rock, Ark., this firm has ceased operations.

In July 1943, the *Crockery and Glass Journal* reported that George D. Rumrill died on April 20.

George Rumrill Dead

George D. Rumrill, owner of the Rumrill Pottery Company, died April 20th, at his home in Little Rock, Arkansas.

He is survived by his wife, a son, Lt. Jack W. Rumrill of the United States Army, and a sister, Miss E. F. Rumrill, who had been associated with him in business for many years.

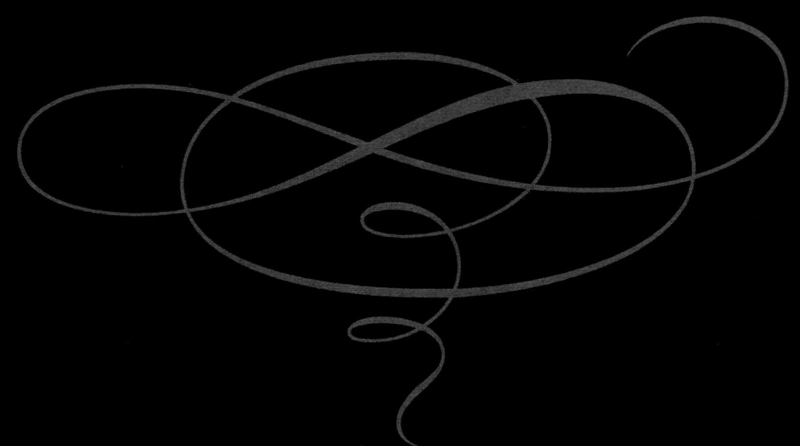

Letters and Interviews

A Letter from Guy Cowan to George Rumrill

One of the people Rumrill wanted to recruit to work at his new pottery line in Ohio was Guy Cowan. Here is a letter Cowan wrote Rumrill turning down the position (courtesy of the Cowan Pottery Museum, Rocky River, Ohio).

November 2, 1937

Mr. George D. Rumrill
Rumrill Pottery Co.
Little Rock, Ark.

Dear Mr. Rumrill:

Your letter of October 27 does not, I am afraid, provide a basis for our getting together on a proposition. I appreciate very much your attitude toward whatever ability I may have.

My position here has many compensations in spite of the fact that there is not very much creative art work to it. However, I have been able to do about the only new things which have been done in the hotel china business, and at the same time been able to make money for our firm.

The chief advantage here is that I am working for the most prosperous and successful firm in this field, and can count on an income above which you consider high, for as long as I live.

One is always taking a chance that new ventures will not live (most of them do not), or that the new surroundings will not prove congenial. However, those are the chances that one must take if a new venture looks promising.

In moving to Syracuse, I felt that I was isolated from the art world that I enjoyed. During these five years it has been possible to bring the center of the ceramic art world to this city. For five years we have had here the National Ceramic Art Exhibitions. From here the Exhibitions have toured the country, being shown in the major European Museums, and which is now being shown, on its return, in New York at the Whitney Museum. See the December issue of Fortune for a story of this work. We have had two of the last three conventions of the Art Division of the American Ceramic Society in Syracuse, and just last week opened a new and beautiful Art Museum, of which I am a trustee and secretary, and which is specializing in ceramic art development.

All of these advantages I would lose if I moved permanently and devoted all my time to work in a section of the Country such as Little Rock. That is the reason why I said that I would consider a proposition which would enable me to spend a part of my time in the art centers and carry on such activities.

In carrying on these activities there is considerable prestige to a firm which uses my name. That is the reason why my present firm is interested in having me carry on. There is also a great deal of stimulation and the possibility of getting many new ideas while working with the leading artists and designers of the Country.

Perhaps from a strictly commercial standpoint, I put too high a value on my name, but I do have considerable pride in what the name Cowan has meant in the past, and I believe still means. That pride would never allow me to have my name on a product which was below the standard I have set for myself.

All of this I have told you, so that you may understand my situation. From that you might be able to work out some proposition which would tempt me to make a change.

Yours sincerely,

R. Guy Cowan

An Interview with Louise Bauer

I personally interviewed Louise Bauer in the summer of 1996 which was a few years before she passed away. Louise was always very ill. The dust in the factories was always a problem for her. Even when she left to start her own company, her studio was always dusty. Although she never admitted it, she obviously suffered from some sort of respiratory disorder. She could never plan any day; it all depended on how she felt that morning. It was very hard to get together with her, but through my persistence and her desire to be quoted, we somehow managed to find the time.

Louise was extremely protective of her material and stated several items that she made during her career were stolen when she allowed strangers into her home. She designed an arrowhead for Shawnee Pottery, and this was her most prized possession. It was always on display at her home, but one day she returned from a shopping trip with her sister and it was gone.

Below is a summary of the interview with her from the summer of 1996.

Louise Bauer, born July 29, was turning 82 that year. She profiled her life from the time she was a little girl to then. Louise Bauer was one of the most gifted designers of her time, and she worked for George Rumrill. She designed a line of vases, miniatures and the Sherry-Louise dinnerware line. The dinnerware line was named after Louise Bauer and Sherry Rumrill, the adopted daughter of Frances Rumrill, George's sister.

Louise remarked how much Rumrill believed in her and how he prompted her to leave Shawnee to start her own business. He was the first person to suggest that her talents were being wasted at Shawnee and that she would be much happier on her own. Louise remarked that Shawnee was paying her "next to nothing" and, against her family's advice, left Shawnee to start her own freelance company. Little did she know that George Rumrill was ultimately responsible for planting the seed that would change American pottery.

It was at this point in her life that she began to utilize all of her talents and creativity. Louise worked long hours in her studio with her brother and father. She enjoyed working with her family and being close to them. Her brother would make her laugh throughout the day and was always kidding about something.

Working at home afforded Louise the opportunity to enjoy the things she liked most: roller skating, bowling, baseball, and other sports. Although she had more work than she could almost handle, she would always factor in some time for herself. She never married.

She described how Rumrill would frequently visit her and hand her sketches of vases he was interested in having her "model up." "He would tell me to take a little more off here on the handle until he liked it," she claimed.

She would also think of new ideas while on vacation. She remembered that the "shell and mermaid" line was conceived while vacationing in the Bahamas and Puerto Rico.

She described George Rumrill as a "very nice man" and "very easy to work for." He would send her to every trade show she wanted: Pittsburgh, Chicago, New York, and other upscale cities.

Besides creating many of the post-Red Wing RumRills that we know today, Miss Bauer also worked for Hull, Gonder, Disney, and others.

Miss Bauer also created the Shawnee trademark, of which she stated she was never given credit.

An Interview with Harry O. Rumrill

At the time of this interview, May 20, 1996, Harry Oliver Rumrill was 89 years old and living in Seminole, Florida. He worked for the RumRill Pottery Company from May to October 1941. Below is a summary of my interview with him.

Harry Rumrill met George Rumrill while George was on business in Chicago. George looked Harry up in the phone book. He called Harry's residence and Harry's wife Katherine gave George Harry's office telephone number. George called Harry up at work and asked to have lunch with him at the Palmer House. Lunch turned into dinner and George Rumrill called Harry's wife and asked her to join them for dinner. When Katherine Rumrill arrived by cab, she noticed both men had been drinking heavily and took her husband home with her in the cab.

When George Rumrill got back to Arkansas, he called Harry and asked Harry to work for him as a salesman. Harry was working for General Electric in the x-ray department at the time but took George up on his offer. He was 34 years old and had already worked 12 years at GE when he decided to make this career move.

Harry did not draw a salary but was on a "drawing account." He was allotted $100 per week which was to include all meals, hotels, and other costs associated with being on the road. In addition, Harry was to have been paid a commission at the end of each year based on the RumRill pottery he had sold during the year.

Harry described George Rumrill as a likeable person and a comedian of sorts. George Rumrill reminded Harry of his father as he always had a good story to tell and was very entertaining. As with the other people I have interviewed, George Rumrill loved to drink and Harry said "he drank the cheapest booze he could get.... Cream of Kentucky."

Harry was in charge of three states: Ohio, Indiana, and Illinois. He would set up in the "sample rooms" at the best hotels in the cities. These hotels would furnish salesmen with skirted tables to display their merchandise. Buyers from major department stores, gift shops, and other stores would visit the hotels, see the merchandise, and place their orders with the salesmen. Some of these buyers were from the May Company, Montgomery Ward, and other stores.

When traveling from one city to the next, Harry would also call on small gift shops to sell them RumRill pottery.

Harry carried several boxes of sample pottery with him at all times. One day while on business in Toledo, Harry got a telegram from the RumRill Pottery Company. The telegram stated that the Florence Pottery Company had burned down in a fire and that all samples of pottery in his possession needed to be returned to the Palmer House in Chicago. The Palmer House was the only hotel in Chicago at the time. Reluctantly, Harry returned the boxes and was out of a job. He was also out any commission on the pottery that was sold during the time he worked in 1941.

Harry Rumrill described David Fisk as an "easterner" and the only Jewish salesman that worked for RumRill Pottery.

Resources

Joe Brawley, collector and author

Ron Hoopes, *The Collector's Guide and History of Gonder Pottery*, L-W Book Sales, Gas City, Indiana, 1992

Ray Reiss, *Red Wing Art Pottery, Including Pottery Made for RumRill*, PROPERTY, Chicago, Illinois, 1996

Myrna Wall, Trustee, Morrow County Historical Society

Cleveland Public Library, archived *Crockery and Glass Journals, Gift and Art Buyer,* and other literature dated 1937 – 1943

Ceramic Industry, May 1938

Ohio Historical Society factory photo, catalog copies, and newspaper articles

Morrow County Historical Society documents and letter from 1939 – 1941, Florence Pottery catalog, price guides, and blueprint for patented feeder arm

United States Patent and Trademark Office, information regarding the transfer of the RumRill trademark to Red Wing, and the assignment back to RumRill Pottery Company

The Federal Bureau of Investigation: research concerning claims made by people interviewed by the author who claimed they were interviewed by the FBI concerning the fire and their accounts of the story. No FBI file existed on Lawton Gonder according to information acquired from the FBI in 1996.

RumRill Catalogs, 1938, 1940, 1940 (Modern Line), 1941 (First Printing), 1942 (Second Printing), 1942

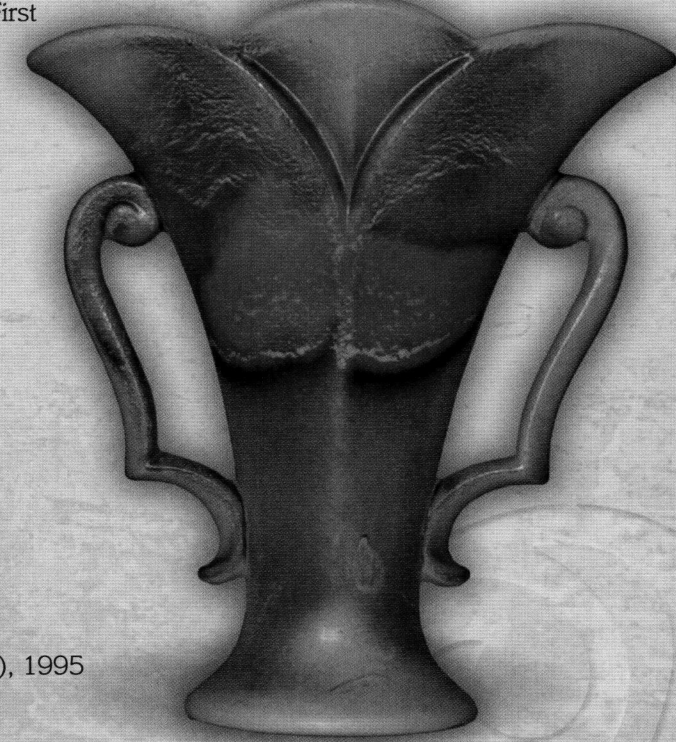

Gonder Catalog, 1943

Cowan Pottery Museum, Rocky River, Ohio

Morrow County Sentinel newspaper

Marion Star newspaper

Interview with Harry O. RumRill, May 20,1996

Interview with Louise Bauer, summer 1996

Interview with Harold West, 1996

Interview with Katherine Kline, 1996

Interview with Evelyn Taylor, 1995

Interview with Georgine Mickler (daughter of George Rumrill), 1995